Critical Guides to Spanish Texts

35   Fray Luis de León: The Original Poems

Critical Guides to Spanish Texts

EDITED BY J.E. VAREY AND A.D. DEYERMOND

FRAY LUIS DE LEÓN

The Original Poems

Elias L. Rivers

Professor of Spanish
State University of New York
Stony Brook, Long Island

Grant & Cutler Ltd *in association with*
Tamesis Books Ltd 1983

© Grant & Cutler Ltd
1983
ISBN 0 7293 0153 2

I.S.B.N. 84-499-6349-4

DEPÓSITO LEGAL: V. 1.848-1983

Printed in Spain by
Artes Gráficas Soler, S.A., Valencia
for
GRANT & CUTLER LTD
11 BUCKINGHAM STREET, LONDON, W.C.2

Contents

for Georgina

... mis faltas supliréis con vuestra sobra,
y vuestro bien hará durable el mío.

Preface

The poetry of Fray Luis de León has long had an immediate appeal for the English-speaking reader, more immediate than most poetry written in Spanish during the sixteenth and seventeenth centuries. A classical diction and a Platonic mode of thought make his poetry relatively accessible, both esthetically and intellectually, to the reader of Spenser and Sidney, of Wordsworth and Shelley. And yet Fray Luis is very Spanish at the same time that he seems to be universal; autobiographical references and details of his use of the Spanish language frequently need to be clarified in ways that will be emphasized in the following pages.

For the English student, Edward Sarmiento's edition of Fray Luis's poetry, published in Manchester in 1953, is the most easily obtainable reliable text; his notes on the poems are succinct and helpful. But, though Sarmiento has modernized the spelling of the first edition (1631), for some reason he has not modernized the punctuation, and this often causes the reader unnecessary problems. For this and other reasons I shall refer primarily to Oreste Macrí's text, published in Salamanca in 1970, with references to Sarmiento's, if different, in parentheses. The detailed commentaries by Sarmiento and Macrí, which I often take for granted and sometimes refer to explicitly, are always found in their footnotes to the lines under discussion. Italic numerals in parentheses refer to the Bibliographical Note. Where necessary they are followed by a page number: (*22*, 150).

My reading of Fray Luis's poetry has been influenced by Dámaso Alonso more than by anyone else; this will be evident in what follows.

Stony Brook, Long Island
September, 1982

Elias L. Rivers

1. Introduction

Though a classical poet like Fray Luis de León strives for timeless perfection, he is inevitably involved in history: his language and his world view are conditioned by his experiences as a child, as a reader of poetry, as a member of society. Fray Luis's poetry, though in some sense remarkably intelligible without reference to these experiences, cannot be fully understood, in all its allusive detail, without a knowledge of the intellectual and political environment within which the poet was active.

We may prefer to think that Fray Luis's partially Jewish ancestry was not important. He, like Santa Teresa, seems to have been unaware of fifteenth-century family conversions. But such descendants of converts as Santa Teresa and Fray Luis often turned out to be combative reformers within the sixteenth-century Spanish church. Perhaps family tradition did reinforce Fray Luis's interest in Hebrew and his belief in the *veritas hebraica*, that is, the priority of the Hebrew text over the Latin Vulgate translation of the Old Testament. And the fact that his maternal great-grandmother had been disciplined by the Inquisition in 1512 for judaizing may well have contributed to his own vulnerability when he was accused before the Inquisition.

Luis's father, Lope de León, was a member of a distinguished family of lawyers living in Belmonte, a town in the Castilian region of Cuenca. Luis was the oldest son, born there in 1527 or 1528. His father's career took the family to Madrid in 1533. When in 1541 his father was appointed to a judgeship in Granada, Luis was sent to the University of Salamanca to study law, but there he soon joined a community of Augustinian monks as a novice and took his formal vows in January of 1544, at the age of sixteen or seventeen. We can be sure that his vocation was fully as intellectual as it was religious. He studied theology for years with the best professors at Salamanca and at Alcalá de Henares, the Spanish Renaissance center of Christian humanism. In 1560 he took his advanced degrees and became eligible for a professorship; he won his first chair a year later. His radical scholarly and theological tendencies first become documentable at this time when, at the request of a nun, he translated from Hebrew into Spanish, with the Church's permission, the Biblical Song of Solomon, a primary text for Christian mystics.

Renaissance humanism had begun as a scholarly return to the primary Greek and Latin sources of the classical tradition, by-passing the Middle Ages. When applied to Biblical scholarship, humanistic textual criticism was equally revolutionary in attempting to get at the original Hebrew and Greek sources of the Christian tradition. Erasmus's edition of the New Testament in Greek and the Polyglot Bible published in Alcalá de Henares had marked the establishment of a strong tradition of Christian humanism in northern Europe and in Spain. Fray Luis de León, along with two scholarly colleagues at Salamanca, attempted to continue this tradition. They strongly supported the publication in Salamanca of an innovating Biblical commentary which had first been published twenty-five years previously in Paris. This led to conflicts with Dominican colleagues, who were generally more conservative than the Augustinians; these Dominicans accused the reformers of being judaizers. Such an accusation was particularly dangerous in Spain, where a special national Inquisition had been in operation for almost a hundred years, policing the Christian orthodoxy of the many families converted from Judaism. In March of 1572, on the basis of Dominican accusations of heresy, Fray Luis de León and his two fellow-professors were imprisoned by the Inquisition and taken to Valladolid, where his trial lasted for almost five years.

We cannot here go into all the technical details of Fray Luis's trial, which are fully documented, for the Inquisition kept scrupulous records of every aspect of accusation and defense. Suffice it to say that Fray Luis's combative and tenacious self-defense, during five years of solitary confinement and without a lawyer, was an extraordinary performance; he stood alone against many equally tenacious accusers. Perhaps because of his delicate health, he was not formally submitted to torture, but he did suffer physically, mentally and spiritually: he was deprived of the Sacraments and of adequate food and lodging. But he finally obtained books, paper and candles. He worked on his own defense with the legalistic mind of a true lawyer. He also studied and wrote. And he finally won an acquittal and returned triumphantly to his university, in December 1576.

A lesser man would have been frightened into submission by such an experience. But Fray Luis had faced the worst and won. Despite the danger of further accusations and trials, he competed for the chair of Sacred Scriptures and won it finally in 1579. And with the security of tenure he began publishing immediately. By supporting Jesuits against Dominicans on the question of free will, he again provoked enemies, who denounced him to the Inquisition in 1582; this time he was not imprisoned, and he was absolved again two years later, with a friendly admonition urging him to avoid polemics. His professional writings were of course in Latin: scholarly Biblical translations and commentaries, several of which were published during his lifetime, but read only by fellow theologians. Obviously he also wanted to reach a larger audience, to bring the Spanish-reading public into closer contact with the Bible. But it was illegal to publish Spanish translations of the Bible. So he wrote works in Spanish based on the Bible: *La perfecta casada*, a treatise on the ideal wife, and *De los nombres de Cristo*, a lively dialogue which presents in attractively readable form a complete doctrine of Christ and human salvation. He also wrote in Spanish a double translation, both literal and poetic, of the Book of Job, with an expository commentary; but this major work, reflecting aspects of his own experience of the righteous man's suffering, was not published until the eighteenth century. And he edited the works of Santa Teresa, the Carmelite reformer, whose mystical writing, in simple earthy Spanish, he believed could bring the Spanish people closer to God. In 1591, shortly after being elected Castilian provincial of the Augustinian Order, Fray Luis de León died, fully vindicated.

Fray Luis died without having published his poetry. As a

theologian, he was not supposed to read or write poetry. But he did. He was an adolescent when the first volume of Renaissance poetry in Spanish was published: *Las obras de Boscán y algunas de Garcilaso de la Vega* (Barcelona, 1543). His perfect assimilation of the new Italianate metrics may well indicate an intense early reading of this epoch-making volume. Garcilaso's only Horatian ode (Canción V), written in *liras* (five-line stanzas rhyming aBabB),[1] provided Luis de León with his favorite classical genre and metric form. Certain of Garcilaso's pastoral themes also took root early in Fray Luis's mind. But his assimilation of Garcilaso was selective: pastoral, Platonic and Stoic elements were retained, while Petrarchan, Ovidian and erotic elements were rejected. Garcilaso led him to reread certain classics. Fray Luis's apprenticeship as a writer of Spanish verse involved translating Virgil's *Eclogues* and selections from the *Georgics* as well as from Horace's lyric poetry. And for these translations Garcilaso's poetry was an inspiration and model; according to the views held in the Renaissance, translation, imitation and original creation were all integral parts of the poet's craft. Fray Luis's first poetic publications appeared anonymously, as a part of a commentary upon Garcilaso's poetry, in the scholarly edition (1574) by Francisco Sánchez de las Brozas, Professor of Rhetoric at the University of Salamanca. It is obvious that this humanist, known as 'El Brocense', had been studying for some time the classical sources of Garcilaso's poetry, discussing them with his learned colleagues such as Fray Luis; he admired the latter's translations of Horace's odes and inserted them as a supplement to his annotations wherever possible, attributing them to 'un docto de estos reinos'. Thus began to spread the semi-underground fame of Fray Luis de León as a poet, first published anonymously in this way while he was in the prisons of the Inquisition.

I have deliberately used the term 'semi-underground'. As an Augustinian monk and professor of theology being criticized by more conservative fellow-theologians, Fray Luis could not afford to advertise himself publicly as a poet. To have done so

[1] Lower-case letters indicate heptasyllables (seven-syllable lines), and capitals indicate hendecasyllables (eleven-syllable lines).

would have seemed frivolous and disrespectful. But no doubt, while his friend El Brocense did not mention him by name, he and El Brocense knew that many other colleagues at Salamanca and elsewhere would recognize and admire his scholarly and elegant classical translations from Horace. And sometime before he died, Fray Luis did gather together the manuscripts of all his Spanish poetry, original and translations, and prepare them for a semi-pseudonymous publication. But they were not published until long after his death, by Francisco de Quevedo, in 1631. Quevedo probably used a somewhat imperfect copy of Fray Luis's original manuscripts, including the poet's own dedicatory prologue. But to understand this prologue correctly, we must realize that Fray Luis did not sign it with his own name, as Quevedo and all subsequent editors would have it, but with the semi-transparent pseudonym 'Luis Mayor', to whom the prologue and the poetry itself are rather ambiguously attributed. Dámaso Alonso (*12*) is the critic who has best explicated this prologue, and in my reading of it I now follow him.

'Luis Mayor' is a fictitious literary double invented by the poet Fray Luis in somewhat the same way that Cide Hamete was invented by Cervantes or Tomé de Burguillos was invented by Lope de Vega. A literary double of this sort is not mere fiction, but an ambiguous combination of real, ironic and ideal, or wish-fulfilling, characteristics of the author's own personality. The dedicatory prologue, attributed to the fictitious Luis Mayor, is addressed to a real person, Don Pedro Portocarrero, rector of the University of Salamanca twice (1556-7 and 1566-7), governor of Galicia (1571-80), and eventually archbishop and inquisitor, and a close friend of Fray Luis. Luis Mayor claims that he wrote the poetry during his early youth, whereas Fray Luis actually wrote it during his maturity, that is, after he was forty years old. Luis Mayor claims to be an almost unknown person, whereas Fray Luis was a nationally-known figure, who ideally in some way longed to be able to 'vivir encubierto', in the way that 'Luis Mayor' claims to. But when Luis Mayor speaks of his attitude toward his poetry, he could well be representing overtly Fray Luis's own conscious attitude: it was written, he says, 'más por inclinación de mi estrella que por juicio y voluntad', not because poetry is unworthy of God, but because the Spanish people tends to see the works of genius as symptoms of ambitious pride and presumption; hence the author says he did not wish to recognize his poetry publicly.

In a second paragraph (beginning 'Pero como suele acontecer ...') the fiction becomes more complicated: Luis Mayor says that, since he did not claim his own poetry, it eventually came to be attributed to a well-known religious person, who out of kindness to him did not reject the attribution until, 'fatigado ya con otras cosas que la malicia y envidia de algunos hombres pusieron a sus cuestas —de las cuales Dios le descargó, como se ha parecido—, trató conmigo que, si no me era pesado, le librase yo también de esta carga'. This 'persona religiosa' is obviously Fray Luis de León himself; the reference to his trial and acquittal by the Inquisition is made in terms typical of him. Thus, the semi-fictitious occasion for the preparation of an edition of the poetry is Fray Luis's request that he no longer be accused of writing poetry. The editorial process described by Luis Mayor was no doubt what Fray Luis himself actually did: he collected manuscript copies of his poetry, expurgated them of other people's poetry, and emended their errors, so as to publish them in a three-part edition dedicated to Don Pedro Portocarrero.

Luis Mayor is clearly speaking for Fray Luis when he writes about how difficult it is to make good translations, and about the malleability of the Spanish language. The final reference to 'el que no me conociere por mi nombre' is deliberately ambiguous, to be read differently by different readers, that is, by those who know that Luis Mayor and Fray Luis were one and the same person, and by those who did not.

It is not known why this manuscript was not sent to a printer and published during Fray Luis's lifetime. My own hypothesis is that Portocarrero dissuaded him: such a transparent fiction as I have analyzed would certainly have challenged Fray Luis's enemies, and Portocarrero probably did not wish to become involved as a collaborator and protector of someone who was twice denounced to the Inquisition. In any case, this autograph manuscript, now lost, must have been circulated widely and copied many times. It is the ultimate, if not immediate, source of

Quevedo's edition and, in substance, of all modern editions. Though some variants are of debatable authenticity, the texts critically established in recent years by Vega (*4*), Sarmiento (*3*) and Macrí (*5*) are as close to Fray Luis's final manuscript as any edition that we are likely to have.

Sarmiento's edition (*3*) is based on Part I ('Poesías originales') of the first edition, published, as I have said, in 1631 by Quevedo. But not all of these poems were actually written by Fray Luis: since 1816 critical editors have agreed in rejecting Nos XXIII (*A Nuestra Señora*, 'No viéramos el rostro al Padre Eterno'), XXV (*Del mundo y su vanidad*, 'Los que tenéis en tanto'), XXVI (*Del conocimiento de sí mismo*, 'En el profundo del abismo estaba'), XXVIII (*Epitafio al túmulo del príncipe don Carlos*', 'Aquí yacen de Carlos los despojos') and XXIX (*Canción a la muerte del mismo*, 'Quien viere el suntuoso'). In addition, No. XXVII (*Canción al nacimiento de la hija del marqués de Alcañices*), though authentic, is simply a variant version of IV. This reduces the total number of authentic original poems to twenty-three. And the order in which these poems appear in Quevedo's edition is not very significant or satisfactory, though most editors have followed the same order for lack of any more authoritative one. If we could date their composition with any precision, this would provide an objective basis for ordering the poems, but unfortunately we cannot; scholars vary widely in their hypothetical dating. I have decided to follow, with slight modifications, Dámaso Alonso's hypotheses as the most objectively based: that the poems were all written probably no earlier than 1569 and perhaps no later than 1584, though Fray Luis may well have continued to revise them; and that, on the basis of internal evidence, these twenty-three poems may be divided into three groups (not necessarily chronological: see Alonso, *10*). Since I propose to follow this order in my discussion of the poems, I will list them here in three groups, giving their numbers in the edition of Macrí, as well as those of Sarmiento (*S*) and Vega (*V*), if different.

1. Occasional, Religious and Patriotic Poems
XXII: 'La cana y alta cumbre' (*V* XIII)

II. 'Virtud, hija del cielo'
IV. 'Inspira nuevo canto' (see also *S* XXVII)
VI. 'Elisa, ya el preciado'
XVIII. 'Y dejas, Pastor santo' (*V* XIX)
XX. 'Las selvas conmoviera' (*V* XXI)
VII. 'Folgaba el rey Rodrigo'

2. Poems on Prison and Deliverance

XI. 'Recoge ya en el seno'
XVII. 'Huid, contentos, de mi triste pecho' (*V* XV)
XIX. '¿Qué santo o qué gloriosa?' (*V* XX)
XXI. 'Virgen, que el sol más pura' (*V* XXII)
XII. '¿Qué vale cuanto vee?'
XV. 'No siempre es poderosa' (*V* XVI)
XVI. 'Aunque en ricos montones' (*V* XIV)
XIV. '¡Oh ya seguro puerto!' (*V* XVII)
XXIII. 'Aquí la envidia y mentira' (*S* XXIV)

3. Satirical and Transcendental Poems

V. 'En vano el mar fatiga'
IX. 'No te engañe el dorado'
I. '¡Qué descansada vida!'
X. '¿Cuándo será que pueda?'
VIII. 'Cuando contemplo el cielo'
III. 'El aire se serena'
XIII. 'Alma región luciente'

Each of the next three chapters will be devoted to a poem-by-poem reading of one of these groups.

My emphasis will not be upon the omnipresent classical models, but some mention of these is occasionally inevitable. Of particular importance for many of Fray Luis's poems is the structure of the classical ode. The Pindaric ode in Greek, named after the poet Pindar, had been a solemn hymn written for a public occasion, in which the poet dramatized himself as the preserver of mythic traditions and gnomic wisdom for a social or political group, the audience. Horace in Latin treated the ode somewhat differently, often converting it into a more modest and private lyric. Though he alluded to myth, his themes were frequently not heroic, but dealt in a moderately Stoic or Epicurean way with facets of everyday life, presented humorously, with ironic self-revelation. His long sentences, or rhetorical periods, cut across short stanzas in a linear development, through image to aphorism, in a way that is more rational than musical. Typically, Horace addressed his modest ode to a friend, in a confidential, conversational way.

Fray Luis was thoroughly familiar with the classical ode; he translated one of Pindar's, and twenty-two of Horace's. And his original poems are often imitations, in detail and in general structure, of the classical ode, especially in the Horatian mode. In this he was working within a Renaissance tradition begun by the Italian humanists who, in the fifteenth century, wrote Latin odes, particularly Landino (1424-1504), associated with Ficino's Platonic Academy in Florence, and Pontano (1426-97), founder of the Neapolitan Academy. Later, Bernardo Tasso (1493-1569) became the first to write Horatian odes in Italian, inventing short stanzas with run-on sentences; his psalms were also written in the form of odes. Tasso's experiments undoubtedly inspired Garcilaso's Canción V, the first Horatian ode in Spanish and the most immediate source of formal influence upon the odes of Fray Luis. But we can suspect that Fray Luis was also directly acquainted with the humanistic ode in Latin and with Tasso's odes in Italian.

We cannot ignore this historical dimension of Fray Luis's odes, a dimension which to some modern readers may seem excessively archeological. But I hope to show how Fray Luis's imitations are original, that is, how they are still alive and meaningful in terms of the Spanish language, of the poet's own life and thought, and of the modern reader's experience as a reader. For in literature, as in language and human culture generally, originality is made possible by tradition; originality is, in fact, a new realization of the potentialities of a tradition. And classical traditionalism, in Fray Luis as in Racine, involves a utopian attempt to transcend the particularities of history and to achieve timeless perfection in literature.

2. Poems of Society, Church and State

If Fray Luis de León had a patron, social and literary, it was Don Pedro Portocarrero, the younger son of a noble family with connections in Belmonte. As a younger son, Don Pedro did not marry, but became a clergyman, and in this capacity served the church and state as university rector, cathedral canon, provincial governor, archbishop and inquisitor general. Obviously he was in a position to help and protect an Augustinian monk. As we have seen, the manuscript 'edition' of Fray Luis's verse was dedicated to Portocarrero; so was the printed edition of *Los nombres de Cristo* (Salamanca, 1583). And within the collected poetry of Fray Luis, three odes are addressed specifically to Portocarrero, two early ones written on public occasions, in the more Pindaric or panegyric mode, and one later, and more intimate, more Horatian ode.

Poem XXII (*V* XIII: 'La cana y alta cumbre') is among the earliest dateable poems by Fray Luis, written in late 1569 or early 1570, during the Morisco revolt in the Alpujarras, in the region of Granada. Two heroes are praised: Don Pedro Portocarrero (or Porto Carrero), addressed in the second person, and his brother Don Alfonso, whose military exploits during the taking of Poqueiro (13 January 1569) are narrated in the third person (lines 50-74). As in most of Fray Luis's odes, the syntactic and rhetorical structure of the poem as a whole is complex, but clear. Each stanza (in this case consisting of six lines, rhyming aBabcC) is a syntactic subdivision, a phrase or clause, but not a complete sentence; and if the poem is punctuated properly, only two or three of the thirteen stanzas end with full stops. Thus the reader is led to move on from stanza to stanza, punctuating mentally as he discovers subordinate and main verbs. Classical, that is Latinate, vocabulary may cause some problems: 'Ilíberi' for the Sierra Elvira or Nevada of Granada, 'Catalina fuente' for the Hippocrene fountain of the Muses, and a few other such words are annotated by the editors. More subtle is the etymological word-play of 'contiene' (line 3) and 'detiene' (line 6): the Sierra Nevada, says the poet, 'contains' your bright presence and thereby 'detains' our joy, which will be renewed when you return. The poem as a whole begins with a contrast between the joys of presence and the sadness of absence (23-4) and ends with a plea for Don Pedro's return from war to peace. His absence of almost one year is referred to as 'ya casi un siglo entero' (4): a semantic Latinism ('siglo' for 'año') coincides here with affective hyperbole.

The praise of Don Pedro, implicit in the joys of his presence, is made explicit with respect to his ancestry and, even more emphatically, his own action and virtues. War is an evil which has assaulted him in the midst of peace (25-6). Mars, the god of war, is personified as the awakener of anger in the hearts of the barbarous infidels. Here the poet's attitude is orthodoxly nationalistic (stanzas 6-7): the Moriscos are bloodthirsty Muslim unbelievers who should not have been so naïvely spared and baptized without sincere conversion. Appearances contradict realities (the name 'amigo' conceals the 'enemigo', in antithetical rhyme, exacerbating the situation); hence the paradoxical oxymoron of 'pïedad crüel', with its emphatic diereses, meaning that Christian pity was in the long run cruel, to Christians as well as to Moriscos. The instability of the situation is summed up in the word 'fortuna', meaning primarily the changeable nature of human affairs and secondarily the outbreak of a storm. The image of war as a storm is fully developed in stanza 8, the climax of the first part of the poem:

> ansí la luz, que agora
> serena relucía, con nublados
> veréis negra a deshora,
> y los vientos alados
> amontonando luego
> nubes, lluvias, horrores, trueno y fuego.

The 'horrores' are literal human atrocities surrounded by metaphorical natural disasters.

The second part of the poem, stanzas 9-13, is a single sentence broken by a long parenthesis extending from line 50 to line 74; in line 74 the 'mas tú' of line 49 is repeated as a syntactic reminder to the reader. This sentence sets up an antithesis between the two brothers. Literally, 'Mas tú que solamente / temes al claro Alfonso ...' means that the only person braver in war than Don Pedro is his brother Don Alfonso. Within the parenthesis, which is a complex relative clause describing Alfonso, we have a miniature epic poem complete with simile. There are echoes of Horace, and also of Garcilaso's Eclogue II, in his praise of Don Fernando Alvarez de Toledo, the militant Duke of Alva. There is no irony in this parenthetical narrative itself, with Don Alfonso, alone and pierced by poison arrows, beating off infidel hordes. But the main clause of the sentence, completing the context, is an argument that if the warrior is great, the peaceful saint is even greater. Thus the final words:

> abraza el ocio santo:
> que mucho son mejores
> los frutos de la paz, y muy mayores.

This is the climax of the poem as a whole, an authentically Christian call to return from the battlefield to the cloister.

The other public ode dedicated to Portocarrero can also be dated by internal evidence: it was written a year or two later, upon the occasion of Don Pedro's becoming governor (regent or 'oidor de la audiencia') of Galicia in 1471. Poem II ('Virtud, hija del cielo') is rhetorically addressed, not to Portocarrero himself, but to Virtue, in the second person; the new governor of Galicia appears in third-person narrative toward the end of the first half of the poem, and this narrative continues through the penultimate stanza. The eighth and final stanza is an exclamation concerning the good fortune of Galicia's inhabitants to be ruled by such a man.

'Virtue', then, is the keynote of this poem. The word itself combines the ancient pagan and Renaissance meaning 'manliness' with the Christian meaning of 'moral quality'. This combination seems particularly appropriate for theocratic

Spain, where, without clear separation of church and state, the king named all bishops and used clerics as his viceroys. The first stanza is the most abstract characterization of virtue. Virtue's source is heaven, that is, God. Line 2 is more complicated: 'empresa' may mean 'undertaking', but in this context, the word's other meaning of 'heraldic emblem' or 'symbolic adornment' seems at least equally appropriate, especially as reinforced by the visual implications of 'ilustre'. Virtue then is a light which descends from bright heaven to dark earth, illuminating man's way. Hercules ('Alcides') at the crossroads chose the narrow, difficult path of virtue and hence, when he died by fire on Mount Oeta, was raised to heaven as a hero. The Spanish poet puts the Cid on a par with Hercules, and Gonzalo Fernández de Córdoba, the conqueror of Italy, on a par with the mythic twins Castor and Pollux. In this we can see how Renaissance poets mythologized their own national heroes by putting them into the same context as ancient heroes. All of this prepares the way in this poem for the apotheosis of Portocarrero, who has chosen 'el bien', 'the good' of Plato's dialogues.

The second half of the poem begins with the austerely aristocratic nature of Portocarrero's virtue: he separates himself ('se descuesta') from the majority of men by scorning money, that is, bribes; he is steadfastly just, undeterred by threats or pleas. Stanza 6 uses the images of arrow and cannonball to characterize the swift and undeviating justice of Portocarrero as a judge:

> Ni mueve más ligera
> ni más igual divide por derecha,
> el aire, y fiel carrera
> o la traciana flecha
> o la bola tudesca un fuego hecha.

The word 'igual', both here and in line 32, is associated with equity: the swift missile traces a straight line dividing the air into two equal parts. The word-order of this stanza shows a Latinate density. In the first line 'ligera' anticipates the feminine singular of 'flecha' and 'bola' in the last two lines. More difficult is the hyperbaton of the second and third lines: 'el aire', instead of being divided, itself as a word divides 'por derecha' and 'y fiel carrera' into two almost equal parts. Certainly the violence of this division on the linguistic level reflects in some way the violence of ancient arrow and modern cannon ball flying through the air.

Galicia, in stanza 7, is seen as a barbarous province being civilized by Castilian government; Portocarrero brings the light of virtue. The final stanza is an anti-climax: nothing new is added except periphrastic specifications of Galicia as a geographical area. (Dámaso Alonso has shown how this sort of anti-climax in Fray Luis's odes is typical of Horatian classicism.) We are left contemplating landscapes: the river Miño, the Atlantic Ocean, the land which stretches from 'la fiel montaña' (Auseba, with the cave of Covadonga, where Don Pelayo began the Reconquest) to 'el fin de la tierra' (the Cape of Finisterre). The final line contains one of those subtle semantic Latinisms noted by Rafael Lapesa in both Garcilaso and Fray Luis: 'desprecia' does not mean 'despises', but 'looks down upon from above', the etymological meaning of the Latin verb 'despicere'. We end, thus, with the high mountains looking down upon the fortunate inhabitants of Galicia; literally this geographical detail has nothing to do with Portocarrero, but metaphorically, in an indirect way, those mountains do represent the heights of his virtue, which is the theme of the ode.

Poem IV, entitled *Canción al nacimiento de la hija del marqués de Alcañices*, is the only other ode, also early (the child was born in January of 1569), concerned with an aristocratic family occasion. The invocation of the epic muse Calliope is justified by the illustrious history of the Borja (Borgia) family; the infant Tomasina's parents were Don Alvaro de Borja and Doña Elvira Enríquez. The child is seen platonically as a gift from Heaven. A playful tone, appropriate to childhood, is set by stanzas 2 and 3, in which the poet asks the sun either to come and see his competitor, or else to allow her to shine in his stead. From stanza 4 on, it is the child's soul that is addressed directly, first by the poet himself and then (beginning with stanza 8) by Apollo, the sun-god of poetry. The soul is seen as descending from Heaven through the planetary spheres to earth, robbing the spheres of their wealth as she passes through; Jupiter, the god of the sixth sphere, and Venus, the goddess of the third, have given her power and beauty, while Saturn and Mars have turned away, sparing her from old age and strife.

The soul is escorted to earth by Apollo, whose song is a poem within the poem. In typically Platonic terms, birth is envisioned as the joining of soul to body. The soul is urged on, in the second person, and the body is referred to, in the third, as waiting in the womb for the soul. The body (stanza 9) represents earthly glory: distinguished ancestors who include two popes in Rome (Callixtus III and Alexander VI) and various crowned heads in Spain (Alfonso XI, Doña Juana Enríquez, Ferdinand the Catholic). The soul (stanza 10) brings to the body heavenly moral virtues. In stanzas 11 and 12, body and soul are incited to merge: the body's beauty is to be seen in the soul's face, and the soul's eyes are to summon mortals to immortality; the body, like a transparent container, is to radiate upon the world the virtuous light of the soul's grace. All previous women of the family, no matter how virtuous and beautiful, will be eclipsed by Tomasina, as fictitious prefigurations are eclipsed by fully revealed truth. The paradoxes of courtly love appear briefly in stanza 15:

> ¡Ay tristes, ay dichosos,
> los ojos que te vieren! Huyan luego,
> si fueren poderosos,
> antes que prenda el fuego,
> contra quien no valdrá oro ni ruego.

Do the poem and Apollo's song end simultaneously with the following stanza? The punctuation in most modern editions would indicate this reading. But the change of tone, from climactic stanza 15 to anticlimactic stanza 16, might well be reinforced by a change from Apollo's voice to that of the poet. The fusion of body and soul, which is Apollo's theme, is complete with the men's eyes that will fall in love with Tomasina's beauty and virtue. The final stanza introduces a change of imagery, a concluding imperative to the young plant to grow in happiness. The poet seems to me to be speaking here *in propria persona*, in a sort of *envoi*.

In Poem VI (*De la Magdalena*) we find a merging of pagan and Biblical motifs which is typical of Fray Luis's syncretism, his combination of different traditions. The first part of the poem (lines 1-30) is largely a classical variation on the Horatian 'carpe diem' (seize the day) commonplace; the rest of the poem treats in a traditional Christian way the penitent figure of St Mary Magdalene.

In its primary form the 'carpe diem' motif is an argument urged by a lover upon a young lady that she should make the best of her youth by enjoying love as soon as possible; that if she does not, she will regret it in her old age, when no man will find her attractive any longer. The vengeful variation found in some of Horace's odes is an 'I told you so' of the sort that Fray Luis develops here in a moralizing direction; in fact, the righteous preacher is almost vindictive in a way that parallels that of the scorned lover. The name Elisa has classical echoes (Virgil, Garcilaso); so has the imagery of golden hair touched by snow. But the preacher's advice had of course been the opposite of 'carpe diem'; it was 'Recoge, Elisa, el pie, que vuela el día', 'Turn back from the way of perdition, for time flies'. The argument, and the description of the aged and abandoned woman, in stanzas 2-5, is predominantly classical, based not so much on Christian morality as on enlightened self-interest. Men's promises of undying devotion have yielded to disgust with wrinkled forehead and blackened tooth; and the old hag suffers. Anaphora (that is, the repetition of a phrase at the beginning of each stanza) and abrupt syntactic enjambement between stanzas 4, 5 and 6 express the cumulative violence of betrayal, lost virginity, vain self-sacrifice, and replacement by another woman. But there are also touches of Platonic morality in such details as 'el alma hecha sierva a vicio bruta' (15). And a major transition begins with stanza 7:

> ¡Oh cuánto mejor fuera
> el don de hermosura, que del cielo

> te vino, a cuyo era
> habello dado, en velo
> santo guardado bien del polvo y suelo!

It would have been much better to have given the heavenly gift of beauty to Him to Whom it belonged ('a cuyo era' is obscurely elliptical in its syntax), protected in a holy veil from dust and dirt. The reference to God and to becoming a nun here shifts from general moralizing to specifically Christian doctrine.

With stanza 8, Christian repentance is presented as a solution that is available as long as there is life. The act of repentance can transform suffering into rest, lust into divine love, as in the case of the Magdalene, who achieved a salvation denied to the falsely self-righteous Pharisee. The poet turns from preaching to narrative as he tells her story and dramatizes her prayer in evangelical terms, those of the gospel according to St Luke (chapter 7). The washing of Christ's feet, forgotten by the Pharisaic host, is performed by anointing hands, kisses and weeping eyes. The near-erotic intensity of this scene is fully realized by the poet, who uses the word-play and paradox of traditional Biblical exegesis (stanza 13):

> Lavaba larga en lloro
> al que su torpe mal lavando estaba;
> limpiaba con el oro,
> que la cabeza ornaba,
> a su limpieza, y paz a su paz daba.

The first line of this stanza sounds like a sob when read aloud. (The word 'larga' is used in the Latin sense of 'abundant, generous'.) And while she was washing Christ's feet physically, He was washing her spiritually clean of sin. With the gold of her hair she cleansed the source of her cleanliness; and she gave the kiss of peace ('paz') to the Prince of Peace. The emotional tone of this passage reminds us of the Reformation, both Protestant and Catholic, which rediscovered the sentimental vitality of the New Testament and re-expressed it in sixteenth- and seventeenth-century poetry and art.

The final five stanzas of this poem are put into the mouth of Mary Magdalene as she makes her plea to Christ. Again, we cannot ignore the intense erotic implications of the situation: those sinful hands and eyes and lips which had been the tools of the prostitute are now offered to Christ, for sin itself provides paradoxically the means of salvation. The lustful fire of her deadly blazing eyes becomes the cleansing water of her tears. She finally presents herself as mortally ill so that the great Physician can have an opportunity to show His healing power to the world for all time.

Biographical interpreters of Poem VI have tried to invent for the role of Elisa an historical Spanish lady, who refused Fray Luis's advice to become a nun as a girl and who, mistreated by a man, was later urged to repent. But the figure of Elisa, no doubt Spanish and Catholic, in some sense, seems to be almost as universal as that of St Mary Magdalene. The former has her roots in Horace's poetry as certainly as the latter has hers in the New Testament. The poem that results is a coherent expression of Counter-Reformation piety and sexual morality.

But Poem XVIII (*En la Ascensión*) is undoubtedly superior in its brief economy of movement, its classical perfection of form. Its subject matter is entirely Biblical, St Luke's version of Christ's ascension into heaven, told at the beginning of the Acts of the Apostles. The poet dramatizes the story from the point of view of one of the disciples, who stares upward at the departing Christ. The device of allowing an anonymous disciple to address first Christ, and then in the final stanza the cloud that 'took Him up out of their sight', is very effective as a way of forcing the reader to imagine the scene and action. The disciple's tone is one of constant protest and bereavement. The Good Shepherd is accused of abandoning His flock and taking refuge in Heaven:

> ¿Y dejas, Pastor santo,
> tu grey en este valle hondo, escuro,
> con soledad y llanto;
> y tú, rompiendo el puro
> aire, te vas al inmortal seguro?

This first stanza, beginning abruptly *in medias res*, conveys an immediate anguish, from a purely human point of view; the future consolation of Pentecost is excluded from the speaker's ken. The deep dark valley of earth-bound life is contrasted with etherial flight through the bright air to a distant region of permanent security. But the speaker, the indirect narrator who is presented as neither omniscient nor reliable, provides the reader with a basic point of view.

In the second stanza, the speaker, identifying himself with the other disciples as a group, uses a third-person plural. (The expected first-person plural does not appear until, very effectively, the last line of the poem.) A basic contrast is set up between past happiness in the presence of Christ and present sadness in dispossession. He has been the sole object of their sensory perception; now, in His absence, upon what can their senses focus? In stanza 3 further rhetorical questions specify first the sense of sight and then the sense of hearing:

> ¿Qué mirarán sus ojos,
> que vieron de tu rostro la hermosura,
> que no les sea enojos?
> Quien oyó tu dulzura
> ¿qué no tendrá por sordo y desventura?

The preterite contrasts with the future, visual 'hermosura' with 'enojos', and audial 'dulzura' with something 'sordo', a 'desventura'. Stanza 4 does not continue the list of the five senses, but rather recalls the miracles of Christ at sea, when He calmed tempests and guided the ship safely to port. He is now imagined as the North Star concealed by a cloud.

The cloud that is suggested metaphorically in stanza 4 is directly addressed, on a more literal level, in stanza 5. Christ is no longer visible, but is 'encubierto'; the protests, therefore, are no longer directed against Him, but against the cloud that conceals Him. This figurative shift from direct to indirect focus (metonymy, or the container for the Person contained) provides the muffled sort of anti-climax which we have seen at the ends of other odes. The cloud is personified as an envious and victorious

competitor with the disciples, rich in contrast with their poverty
and blindness, they being deprived now of their guiding star.

We might well conclude that in this poem Fray Luis de León
chose to combine Biblical content directly with classical form in
order to produce a Christian ode. But there is at least one
mediating influence, that of Ignatius Loyola's *Spiritual
Exercises*. In devotional meditations of the sort prescribed by
the founder of the Jesuits, there was a standard psychological
procedure for using a Biblical scene or episode as an incitement
to religious emotions. This procedure was known as 'composition of place' through 'application of the senses': that is, the
scene was to be imagined as a space in which sensorially percep-
tible events were taking place, and the meditator was to con-
struct that scene in his imagination by trying to perceive in a concrete way the sights, sounds, smells, tastes and tactile sensations
involved in the action. In this *Ode on the Ascension* we can see
the influence of the devotional technique of meditation; the ode
is not, of course, a standard Jesuit 'spiritual exercise', but within
its historical dramatization it does apply the two higher senses to
the perception of Christ's departure. The reader is thereby pro-
jected into the disciple's point of view and, by reading, is led to
imagine the pre-Pentecostal Church's sense of abandonment.
The first and last verb is '¿dejas? ...¡dejas!' The reader experiences vicariously an episode and a spiritual attitude that had
important consequences within the Christian Church and, we
might add, within the personal life of Fray Luis, who, like Job,
knew what it was to cry out, in the face of great adversity, 'My
God, my God, why hast Thou forsaken me?'.

Poems XX and VII are patriotic odes based upon two important figures belonging to the national mythology of Spain:
Santiago Matamoros, or St James the Apostle and Moor-Killer,
patron saint of the Reconquest; and Rodrigo or Roderick, the
last Visigothic king, who lost Spain to the Moors. One stands for
the triumph, and the other for the defeat, of Spain. As a
Christian humanist in the tradition of Erasmus, Fray Luis was
aware that, just as Greece and Rome had epic mythologies that
were drawn upon by poets in their national odes, so Spain too
had its medieval legends, which everyone still knew and most

people still believed, and that they could be drawn upon by the writers of humanistic or neoclassical odes. The classical model for Poem XX is not any one particular poem, but the general type of Pindaric ode (see Chapter 1) celebrating the praise of a god or great hero. Poem VII, on the other hand, is a quite specific imitation of Horace's *Prophecy of Nereus*.

The Spanish legend of St James is summarized in detail by Sarmiento in the notes to his edition (*3*, p.91). Suffice it to say at this point that the apostle was supposed to have preached the gospel in Spain before being beheaded in Palestine. His body was supposedly brought back to Spain by boat and buried somewhere in Galicia; the tomb was miraculously rediscovered in Compostela a hundred years after the Muslim invasion of Spain and eventually became the focal point of an important medieval pilgrim route. (In fact, the crusading French monks of Cluny were responsible for building up this route as a line first of defense and then of offensive military action.) Santiago came to be the anti-Mohammed, the warrior saint seen leading Christians into battle mounted on a white horse. The long text of Poem XX (160 lines or 32 stanzas in Quevedo's edition, and 170 lines or 34 stanzas in some manuscripts) is divided quite clearly into six sections. With the shorter version as our base, the stanzas divide as follows: 1. Introduction (1-2); 2. Martyrdom (4-9); 3. Body's boat journey (10-16); 4. Moorish conquest of Spain (17-22); 5. Christian reconquest of Spain (23-9); 6. Conclusion (30-2).

The introduction and the conclusion, consisting of three stanzas each, provide a lyric or panegyric framework for the central narrative sequence. The poet, in the introduction, wishes that he were an Orpheus so as to be able to celebrate adequately the name of Santiago, his liberation of Spain, and the transportation of his body. In his conclusion, the poet addresses the saint once more, as he often does in the central part of the poem, declaring his sword victorious and his fame world-wide, with pilgrims coming from north and south, east and west.

Santiago's martyrdom is caused by his own emotional closeness to Christ; he wanted to die as soon as possible so as to rejoin his friend and master (stanza 6):

> No sufre larga ausencia,
> no sufre, no, el amor que es verdadero;
> la muerte y su inclemencia
> tiene por muy ligero
> medio por ver al dulce compañero.

For this reason Santiago completed his mission in Spain and returned to Palestine as soon as possible (stanzas 7-8); beheading fulfilled his desires.

After death Santiago sent his body to Spain as a source of light in darkness. At this point the predominant narrative tense shifts from preterite to historical present, which tends to keep the reader in direct contact with the action. One charming touch of pagan mythology makes the voyage near Greece seem strangely playful, as mermaids gaze in amazement and urge one another to help push the boat:

> Por los tendidos mares
> la rica navecilla va cortando;
> Nereidas, a millares
> del agua el pecho alzando,
> turbadas entre sí la van mirando;
>
> y de ellas hubo alguna
> que, con las manos de la nave asida,
> la aguija con la una
> y con la otra tendida
> a las demás que lleguen las convida.

The poet here combines in his imagination a passage from Virgil with another from Catullus, adding perhaps an echo from Garcilaso. From a certain purist point of view, predominant in neo-classical France or Protestant England, mermaids (or sirens, traditionally associated with the Devil) should never be allowed to swim and play near the body of a Christian saint. But in Italy and even Spain, well into the sixteenth century at least, such esthetic homage to pagan antiquity was not felt to be unchristian; Sannazaro's Latin poem on Christ, *De Partu Virginis*, for example, has mermaids playing in the Jordan River. For a Christian humanist like Fray Luis, there seems to have been no conflict between the human truth of classical poetry and the divine truth of the Bible or religious tradition.

We follow the boat from the Aegean to the Ionian Sea, from Sicily to Corsica to the Straits of Gibraltar, where Spain receives her patron saint without any thought of future disaster. But stanza 16, at the end of this section, is a prophecy of invasion and thus a transition to the following section, in which the prophecy is realized in present-tense narration. (As we shall soon see, this entire passage anticipates in theme and technique Fray Luis's Poem VII, *The Prophecy of the Tagus*.) The invasion is visualized in a vividly immediate way, with the sea covered by ships, people swarming on the beaches ('hierve la costa en gente, en sol la arena'), oarsmen shouting. A prayer for Spain is cut off by the swift, predestined defeat that sweeps the country like a flood (stanza 22):

> ¿Cuál río caudaloso,
> que los opuestos muelles ha rompido
> con sonido espantoso,
> por los campos tendido
> tan presto y tan feroz jamás se vido?

But the Reconquest, in the mythological perspective of this poem, begins immediately, under the aegis of Santiago. There is in fact no mention of human Christian soldiers; there is only the superhuman figure of the saint converted into Mars and descending from heaven with his gleaming sword, like a lightning bolt, dazzling and destroying. Again the movement is rapid, violent, merciless (stanzas 25-7):

> De grave espanto herido,
> los rayos de su vista no sostiene
> el moro descreído;
> por valiente se tiene
> cualquier que para huir ánimo tiene.

Huye, si puedes tanto,
huye; mas por demás, que no hay huida;
bebe dolor y llanto
por la mesma medida
con que ya España fue de ti medida.

As we can see in such passages as these, the voice of the poet-narrator is directly involved in the action as he addresses the fleeing Moor and proclaims vengeance and victory: 'y de la gloria estamos en la cumbre.' With this line the narrative ends and the lyric epilogue begins.

The poem to Santiago is certainly Fray Luis's most ambitious Pindaric ode. This genre of poetry may not appeal to modern writers, and it may not seem typical of Fray Luis's best; but as an experiment it is a significant achievement, anticipating in a minor key the grandiose organ voice of Fernando de Herrera's more Biblical ode on the contemporary Victory of Lepanto.

Poem VII, the final poem in our group of public odes, is the most directly imitative of a specific ode by Horace. The relationship between the two poems, Horace's *Prophecy of Nereus* (I, xv) and Fray Luis's *Prophecy of the Tagus*, has been exhaustively studied by Dámaso Alonso (*10*). The loss of Visigothic Spain to Islam was mythically moralized in well-known Spanish ballads: Rodrigo, the last Visigothic king, was said to have raped or seduced a noble damsel named 'la Cava'; her father, Count Julian, in order to avenge himself, called in the Muslims, who crossed the Straits of Gibraltar and destroyed the Visigothic kingdom at the Battle of Guadalete. Fray Luis and other humanists saw the parallel between this story and the classical story of how Paris's abduction of Helen led to the destruction of Troy by the Greeks. Fray Luis may also have recalled a ballad about Rodrigo's prophetic dream (see Vossler, *31*). Horace had condensed and dramatized his story by putting it in the prophetic mouth of the sea god Nereus; Fray Luis invented the river god Tagus (the Visigothic capital was Toledo, on the Tagus River) and performed the proper transformations, imitating many of the stylistic details of the Latin poem. In both poems, the first stanza introduces the speaker, whose words constitute the rest of the poem. But Fray Luis elaborated freely upon the terrible concrete details of war and destruction, with a touch of Old Testament violence alien to Horace; the Spanish poem has more lively movement and variety than the Latin poem has. Dámaso Alonso (*9*, pp.134-54) has also studied in detail the stylistic development of the *Profecía del Tajo* as a poem considered independently of its Latin model. Its formal perfection is comparable to that of Poem XVIII (*En la Ascensión*).

The first line ('Folgaba el rey Rodrigo') of this classical ode on the fall of Spain must have reminded contemporary readers of the first line of various ballads on the same subject: 'Trataba amores Rodrigo' (*31*, 122-3). The first stanza describes the familiar scene in its first three lines and then, in preterite narrative, adds an unfamiliar twist, alien to the ballad tradition: the river suddenly produced a classical river god, identified with the river itself, and spoke. The grotesquely humorous detail of the river (god) sticking his head and shoulders out of the river is comparable to the mermaids of Poem XX (*A Santiago*); the humor is in the syntax itself, for one would expect 'el pecho sacó fuera *del* río', but '*el* río' turns out to be the subject. This touch of humor is part of an ironic framework (Fray Luis did not of course believe literally in river gods) which in no way undercuts the seriousness of the poem's substance.

Dámaso Alonso calls attention to the hyperbaton (displacement of normal word order) and the polysyndeton (repetition of conjunctions) of stanza 2: the verb 'siento' is tucked in among its direct objects, which are linked by one more 'y' than is necessary. The confusion of word order here reflects the initial confusion of the prophetic vision, as does the superfluous conjunction. More important is the present tense of the verb of perception, anticipating the future with the breathless repetition of the adverb 'ya ...ya'. The future is thus actualized, that is, felt to be already present. The relative objectivity of perception in stanza 2 yields to subjective exclamations in stanza 3 and then again to objective nouns in stanza 4. The ironic juxtaposition of opposites is emphasized: sexual delight, a beautiful woman, and an embrace actually involve bitter tears, the fall of a kingdom, and the whole list of woes in stanza 4. The indirect objects of all this (the king himself and his subjects) are slowly elaborated upon in stanza 5; the various regions are summed up and expanded in an impressive final line: 'a toda la espaciosa y triste España.'

After this reflective pause, the tempo picks up again with the 'ya' of stanza 6 and moves toward a crescendo responding to the Count's call for an invasion from Africa: his call is echoed by a trumpet across the straits, flags are unfurled, lances are brandished. Each verb contributes to the military noise and movement, which approach a synesthetic climax in stanza 9:

> Cubre la gente el suelo;
> debajo de las velas desparece
> la mar; la voz al cielo
> confusa y varia crece;
> el polvo roba el día y le escurece.

This objective peak is followed once more by subjective exclamations (stanza 10) and then by the coldly mythological support of the elements (Aeolus is the god of air or wind, Neptune that of water or sea) given to the invading forces.

In stanza 12 the prophetic river god, in the name of Spain, once more addresses King Rodrigo as the morally culpable cause of disaster, calling upon him to rise immediately from his lascivious bed and to take up arms against the invader. A rapid sequence of juxtaposed imperatives fills the lines of stanza 13 without any padding of conjunctions:

> Acude, corre, vuela,
> traspasa la alta sierra, ocupa el llano,
> no perdones la espuela,
> no des paz a la mano,
> menea fulminando el hierro insano.

At this point Oreste Macrí closes the quotation in his edition (5), implying that here the river ceases speaking and that the omniscient poet-narrator begins to close the poem as he had opened it. It is true that in the remaining three stanzas King Rodrigo is no longer addressed; he is in fact completely lost sight of. But this is not sufficient to indicate a change of speaker, especially when the Horatian model has no such change. And in stanza 14 Fray Luis comes close to translating his model literally: 'quantus adest viris sudor' becomes 'cuánto de sudor está presente al que viste loriga'.

But, even though the speaker does not change, in the last two stanzas the River Tagus does address two different personifications: the River Betis (Guadalquivir) and Spain. This does make for a distinct shift of focus, de-escalating, we might say, toward what Dámaso Alonso calls the 'cold' anticlimax of the final stanza 16, which 'shades off toward a paralyzing grief', in Fray Luis as in Horace. The second declarative sentence is broken by two brief emotional exclamations; the cold external form cannot repress, but rather heightens, the deep feeling associated with the great national defeat in a six-day battle (stanza 16):

> El furibundo Marte
> cinco luces las haces desordena,
> igual a cada parte;
> la sexta, ¡ay!, te condena,
> oh cara patria, a bárbara cadena.

When the new second person of 'te condena' is identified by '¡oh cara patria!', the reader feels that something has finally burst through after being repressed throughout the entire ode. After all, the River Tagus and Rodrigo are equally mythological personifications or evasive devices: for the sixteenth-century Spaniard the underlying emotional truth was the new nationalism of Spain, a patriotic love for his country. Hence no doubt Macrí's desire to put this final exclamation into the mouth, not of a river, but of the Spanish poet Fray Luis himself.

The group of seven odes which we have studied in this chapter gives evidence of our poet's involvement in the external world of an ecclesiastical patron who fought Moriscos and governed Galicia, of an aristocratic family with a new-born daughter, of traditional ideas on sexual morality and female repentance, of devotional meditation on Biblical scenes, of the nationalistic myths of Santiago the Moor-Killer and of the Visigothic king whose sexual self-indulgence opened the gates to Moorish invasion and occupation. Dealing with such themes, Fray Luis is an interesting and able poet, but hardly a great one. He becomes much more interesting when he poeticizes his own experience as a prisoner falsely denounced to the Inquisition by unscrupulous enemies and as a strong-willed defender of himself who, with the help of God, wins a favorable verdict.

3. On Prison, Enemies and Deliverance

Poem XI is dedicated to Fray Luis de León's friend and fellow-scholar Juan de Grial, Canon of Calahorra. These two men, as theologians, gave one another intellectual support throughout Fray Luis's career; they were also both interested in poetry, Latin and Spanish. This poem gives some idea of their companionship, interrupted by Fray Luis's imprisonment. The first three stanzas are a tranquil evocation of autumn, sad and dark. In stanzas 4-7 this season is seen as an invitation to study and to the writing of poetry, and Grial is urged to continue developing his style, ignoring vain wealth. In the final line of stanza 7 the poet declares his inability to compete with his friend, but this hardly prepares us for the sudden violence of stanza 8:

> que yo, de un torbellino
> traidor acometido y derrocado
> del medio del camino
> al hondo, el plectro amado
> y del vuelo las alas he quebrado.

What we first notice in this poem is a certain intimacy of tone. This is a private ode, not a public one. Contemplation of the autumn landscape is sensitively melancholy, self-contained:

> Recoge ya en el seno
> el campo su hermosura; el cielo aoja
> con luz triste el ameno
> verdor, y hoja a hoja
> las cimas de los árboles despoja.

In the following stanzas classical mythology is a slight obstacle to the modern reader, but the first stanza is still transparent, and (despite Greek accusative) so are lines 14-15:

y, el yugo al cuello atados,
los bueyes van rompiendo los sembrados.

(By 'Greek accusative' I mean the peculiar syntax of 'el yugo', which we would expect to be governed by a preposition, corresponding to a Latin ablative: 'los bueyes atados [por] el yugo al cuello'.) The essential elements are falling leaves, a change of sun and length of days, windy clouds at midday, the hoarse sound of cranes migrating overhead, oxen plowing. Despite the melancholy tone, there is nothing yet to prepare us for the violence of the final stanza.

An élitist desire for fame, as well as the autumn season, leads scholarly poets into their studies to write. The classical image is one of ascending Mount Parnassus: Grial's firm stride need only be lengthened to win the slope and peak, where he can slake his burning thirst in the fountain of poetry. But there is one potentially ominous note here in line 22: 'solo gana...' It is ambiguous: 'win it alone because you are strong' or 'win it alone because I will not be with you.' In contrast to the thirst-quenching waters of poetry, gold is an empty wind which cannot satisfy the thirst for wealth. It is not clear exactly what lines 32-4 mean; it seems that Grial is to write in a new classical style, probably that introduced by Garcilaso and Boscán, for it equals and surpasses either the old (medieval) style or perhaps even classical antiquity itself.

Again we are struck by the sudden violence of the final stanza: a treacherous whirlwind has snatched the poet from the center of the road up Mount Parnassus and has hurled him into the depths, breaking his musical instrument and his wings of poetic flight. The words 'torbellino traidor' are the only ones that make us sure that the poet is referring to the enemies who denounced him to the Inquisition. Given this context, the 'hondo' becomes not only a metaphor, but the physical depths of a dungeon in Valladolid. And with the breaking of plectrum and wings, the poem, his poetry, ends.

But Fray Luis was eventually able to study and write in prison. Poem XVII, *En una esperanza que salió vana*, is certainly set in the context of imprisonment, probably in 1572, when his hopes for an early acquittal were disappointed. In genre and form this poem is not an ode, in *lira* stanzas, but an elegy, in *terza rima*. The classical elegy, in Greek and Latin, had been defined primarily by its metrical form, the elegiac couplet, a self-contained syntactic unit consisting of a dactylic hexameter (one long syllable, two short, one long, two short) followed by a pentameter, a shorter line. In Italian poetry the most nearly equivalent unit was the hendecasyllabic tercet, or *terza rima*, used from Dante's time onward for more or less satirical poetry. The rhyme scheme may be continued indefinitely, beginning ABA, BCB, CDC... and eventually ending with a four-line group (YZYZ). Some of the earliest poems labelled elegy in Italian were, like the earliest odes, written by Bernardo Tasso. Garcilaso wrote two elegies, both in *terza rima*, one to console the Duke of Alva for the death of his young brother and one to complain to Boscán about the way in which war had separated him from a mistress in Naples. The common denominator seems to be lamentation; but as Claudio Guillén has shown in an important article,[2] elegies, epistles and satires were not clearly separated genres since they all tended to be written in *terza rima* and to express similar themes and attitudes. I have no doubt that Fray Luis was conscious of writing in a classical elegiac tradition, for example, in that of Ovid's *Tristia ex Ponto*; but we may also allow for a measure of satire.

The first line of Poem XVII, 'Hüid, contentos, de mi triste pecho', sets a purely elegiac tone which lasts unbroken for nine tercets (through line 27) as the poet persistently rejects happiness and asserts his hopelessness. The personification of happiness ('contentos') is a rhetorically useful device: the 'contentos' are àccused of self-deception, forgetfulness, a direct antipathy to his own state of mind. He depicts a desolate inner landscape of 'nublados/y viento y torbellino y lluvia fiera'. It is the antithesis of the traditional *locus amoenus*, or bower of love (lines 10-15):

> No pinta el prado aquí la primavera
> ni nuevo sol jamás las nubes dora

---

[2] 'Sátira y poética en Garcilaso', in *Homenaje a Casalduero* (Madrid: Gredos, 1970), pp.209-33.

> ni canta el ruiseñor lo que antes era;
>   la noche aquí se vela, aquí se llora
> el día miserable sin consuelo
> y vence al mal de ayer el mal de agora.

Anaphora, the repetition of 'Guardad vuestro destierro' at the beginning of each of four tercets, brings to an emphatic climax this introductory section of subjective elegiac sentiment.

The second section (28-45) is more objective, with direct references to the counter-productive efforts of the poet to defend himself against his accusers: 'mancíllanse mis manos si se apuran', that is, his hands become stained in self-defense. And although he is innocent, he is punished: 'las culpas faltan, mas las penas duran.' It is his knowledge of his own innocence that makes him suffer most (34-6). He compares himself to the bird that, by trying to get out of the bird-lime, becomes more firmly glued; the world of justice is reversed, for his innocence pays for others' guilt, and the criminal is his jailer and defamer (40-5):

> Cuanto desenlazarse más pretende
> el pájaro captivo, más se enliga,
> y la defensa mía más me ofende.
>   En mí la culpa ajena se castiga
> y soy del malhechor, ¡ay!, prisionero,
> y quieren que de mí la fama diga.

The third section (46-63) is an embittered variation upon the 'beatus ille' motif, which is set in a more positive context in Poem I (*Vida retirada*). The praise of country life is here made directly antithetical to experience of law courts and personal hatreds. Solitude and the simple life bring with them innocence and truth. There seem to be ambiguous references to hand-shackles and prison-bars in the following lines (52-7; the subject is the fortunate man who lives in the country):

> Cuando la luz el aire y tierras baña,
> levanta al puro sol las manos puras
> sin que se las aplomen odio y saña;

> sus noches son sabrosas y seguras;
> la mesa le bastece alegremente
> el campo, que no rompen rejas duras...

(Literally, of course, the 'rejas' are plowshares, which are not necessary for such idyllic agriculture; but surely they remind one of bars in a window too.) A brief four-line epilogue or envoi neatly returns to the rhetorical situation of the introduction: happiness (now 'contento' in the singular) is urged to go live in the country and to deny any knowledge of the poet-prisoner to those that enquire about him:

> Allí, contento, tus moradas sean;
> allí te lograrás; y a cada uno
> de aquellos que de mí saber desean
> les di que no me viste en tiempo alguno.

Dámaso Alonso is right to call our attention to the high quality of Poem XVII, which has been neglected by critics perhaps because its elegiac form is unfamiliar to most readers of Fray Luis's odes. (There is only one other exception, the very familiar *quintillas* of Poem XXIII, *A la salida de la cárcel*.) There is no note of intimacy here; but the combination of elegiac hopelessness, satirical denunciation of accusers, and bitterly ironical 'beatus ille' make this poem one of Fray Luis's major, and most remarkable, accomplishments.

Poem XIX, *A todos los santos*, is a Christian parody, an *a lo divino* version, of a pagan ode. For celebrating All Saints' Day and commenting on the present state of the church, Fray Luis chose as his model an ode (I, xii) in which Horace had celebrated the ancient gods and heroes, invoking Jupiter's blessing upon the Emperor Augustus. But whereas Horace's ode culminates with praise for the Emperor by equating him, second only to Jupiter, with the other gods and heroes of the first part of the poem, Fray Luis's ode culminates with denunciation of the Church for being a corruption of past saintliness. Some scholars (Dámaso Alonso, *11*, among them) have concluded that the first part of the poem was written before Fray Luis's imprisonment and the second part in prison. Such an hypothesis seems to me unnecessary; in fact, 'estas breñas' of line 10 may not necessarily be at odds with 'este estrecho' of line 88. The major formal break in Fray Luis's ode, which Dámaso Alonso explains biographically, corresponds exactly to the major formal break in Horace's ode. Only the last two stanzas of the Augustinian's poem have no antecedent in Horace; they evidently form a postscript of a personal sort, with specific references to his own imprisonment that reinforce his criticism of the Church.

The Christianization of pagan elements is interestingly minimal. Instead of:

> Quem virum aut heroa lyra vel acri
> tibia sumis celebrare, Clio?
> Quem deum?...

Fray Luis begins:

> ¿Qué santo o qué gloriosa
> virtud, qué dëidad que el cielo admira,
> oh musa poderosa
> en la cristiana lira,
> diremos?...

The saintly company of heaven is called heaven's 'caballería'. David replaces Orpheus as the musician who moves woods and animals; Jesus Christ like Jupiter is highest on the list of powers, with the Virgin Mary corresponding to Minerva next in succession. Then, with usually one stanza each, follow St Michael, Saints Peter and Paul (one stanza), St Mary Magdalene, St Catharine of Alexandria, St Augustine, St Jerome, St Ambrose, St John Chrysostom (these last four in a single stanza), St Basil, and finally St Francis of Assisi and St Antony of Egypt (these two in a single stanza). The two pantheons are comparable in length; cryptic periphrasis lends some interest to an orthodox catalogue of mythic figures.

The substance of the poem really begins with stanza 15, in which God the Father is invoked as judge of His Church (compare Horace's 'gentis humanae pater atque custos'):

> ¡Ay Padre! ¿y dó se ha ido
> aquel raro valor? ¡Oh!, ¿qué malvado
> el oro ha destruido
> de tu templo sagrado?
> ¿Quién cizañó tan mal tu buen sembrado?
>
> Adonde la azucena
> lucía, y el clavel, do el rojo trigo,
> reina agora la avena,
> la grama, el enemigo
> cardo, la sinjusticia, el falso amigo.
>
> Convierte piadoso
> tus ojos y nos mira, y con tu mano
> arranca poderoso
> lo malo y lo tirano,
> y planta aquello antiguo, humilde y llano.

Where have all the saints gone? Who has destroyed the best of the Church? These radically critical questions, with line 75, take the form of a familiar parable (Matthew xiii), in which Christ compared the kingdom of heaven to a field first sown with good wheat and later sown, secretly by an enemy, with tares or weeds. Our poet's specific identification of the weeds with 'la sinjusticia, el falso amigo' points toward his own trial. But his prayer for the restoration of the primitive church in all its sanctity was common to many reformers, Protestant and Catholic, of the sixteenth century.

In his personal postscript (stanzas 18-19) he is even more specific:

> Da paz a aqueste pecho,
> que hierve con dolor en noche escura,
> que fuera de este estrecho
> diré con más dulzura
> tu nombre, tu grandeza y hermosura.

This is certainly a prayer for delivery from prison. And in it we see the germ of a basic antithesis which will become more and more important as we study his poetry, developing into an antithesis between darkness and light, earth and heaven. The final stanza is a repentant anti-climax: his sins are even greater than his state of abandonment, but they will eventually redound to the praise of his divine deliverer.

An even more eloquent prayer for delivery is Poem XXI, *A Nuestra Señora*. This poem is an ode of a different kind, modelled on Petrarch rather than on Horace. Petrarch had written a similar *canzone*, or ode, to the Virgin as the final poem in his *Canzoniere*, or collection of *canzoni*, madrigals and sonnets predominantly devoted to the love of a woman, Laura. Fray Luis probably planned to end his collection of poetry in the same way. The Petrarchan stanza is long, in this case eleven lines instead of Fray Luis's usual five or six, and each of the nine main stanzas (but not the short envoi) has a similar syntactic pattern, emphasized by the repetition of 'Virgen' at the beginning of each stanza. For this reason we can say that the development is circular rather than linear; lyrical repetition here predominates over any sequential development of thought or action. In addition to the dominant Petrarchan model, there are echoes of Dante, of classical authors, and of the Bible. There is also an underlying pattern taken from Christian liturgy: we may read each stanza as a collect, or short prayer, with its invocation, of exactly three lines, its petitions and plaints, and frequently a concluding vocative or return to the second person. The form of the collect merges in this way with that of the Petrarchan stanza.

Despite the insistence of some scholars that we should take the 'cárcel' of line 5 as an allegorical reference to earthly life in general, there are many indications throughout the poem that Fray Luis is referring literally to his imprisonment in Valladolid. In the first three stanzas, whose main verbs are petitions in the imperative or subjunctive mood, this is only suggested by such phrases as 'culpa ajena' (line 9), 'el odio cunde, la amistad se olvida' (line 28). But in stanzas 4 to 7 petitions give way to declarative descriptions in the indicative mood; as we decipher the metaphors, their cumulative sense is clearly an indictment of his Dominican accusers. In stanza 4 he is besieged by their 'poder sin ley ninguna'. In stanza 5 he is drowning while people look at him from the shore, unwilling or unable to help him. In stanza 6, truth is naked and helpless, while falsehood is well armed and powerful. In stanza 7 he sees himself as blindfolded and tied to a stake, the target of many arrows:

> siento el dolor, mas no veo la mano,
> ni me es dado el huir ni el escudarme.

These words seem quite specifically related to the prisoner's complaint, made in May of 1573, that he could not defend himself effectively if he did not know who his accusers were.

I have said that the development of this poem is circular or repetitive, rather than linear. This is particularly true of the nine invocations of three lines each, which modern editors should set off by colons. (The tenth shorter stanza, or envoi, reduces its invocation to the single word 'Virgen', without modifiers.) In each of these invocations the Virgin is characterized theologically, devotionally or iconographically: she is seen, for example, as treading upon the moon and the serpent, as consenting to the angel's annunciation, as star of the sea, as immaculately conceived. In stanza 9 the poet declares his lifelong devotion to the Virgin, a devotion referred to also in the *Nombres de Cristo* (under the discussion of 'pimpollo', the first name explicated in Book I): 'atrévome yo a llamarla mía en particular, porque desde mi niñez me ofrecí por todo a su amparo.' This poem is an eloquent expression of the figurative child's yearning for motherly protection under the cruel circumstances of imprisonment and trial for heresy.

Poem XII ('¿Qué vale cuanto vee?') is one of three odes addressed to Felipe Ruiz. We know very little about this apparently important friend, and perhaps relative, of the poet: his full name was Felipe Ruiz de la Torre y Mota, and he wrote poems in Latin, two of which he dedicated to Fray Luis, in 1582 and 1585. In his study of the three odes as a group, Lapesa (22) notes that poem XII begins with the same question that is posed at the end of Poem V (*A Felipe Ruiz: De la avaricia*, 'En vano el mar fatiga'); this indicates the sequence in which they should perhaps be read, leading up to Poem X ('¿Cuándo será que pueda?') as the climax of the group. Because, however, of the overt allusions to prison and vindication in Poem XII, I will continue in this case to follow Dámaso Alonso's classification, as explained in Chapter 1.

The general rhetorical question of the first stanza denounces the common preoccupations of worldly men. (In line 5 'afanar' as a transitive verb poses a problem: is 'la vil gente' the subject or the object? If the latter, we should probably interpolate a preposition: 'afana [a] la vil gente'.) In the following three stanzas these preoccupations are specified as the avaricious hoarding of money, the struggle for power, and the dearly bought joys of love. Each of these 'afanes' is present as a paradoxical self-punishment: while 'pardoning' (in the sense of the Latin verb *parcere*: 'to spare or save'; see Lapesa, *23*) his money, the miser is cruel to himself; the would-be political master must humiliate himself as a fawning slave; and for a brief moment of joy, the lover suffers endlessly before and afterwards.

The rest of the poem stands in proud opposition to the vile slavery of such people. In stanza 5 the poet begins to evoke the self-sufficient Stoic philosopher who fearlessly thrives upon adversity:

> Dichoso el que se mide,
> Felipe, y de la vida el gozo bueno
> a sí solo lo pide,
> y mira como ajeno
> aquello que no está dentro en su seno.

The reflexive pronouns emphasize an inward turning, a rejection of dependence upon external things: the ideal person sets his own standards of self-restraint ('se mide'), makes demands only upon himself ('a sí solo lo pide'), and rejects all that is alien to his inner soul. The words of this stanza, and the following ones, often echo passages from Horace, but we can be sure that Fray Luis felt no contradiction between Horace's 'justum virum' and the righteous man of David's Psalms or the inner man of reformed Christian spirituality.

In stanzas 7 and 8 we find an emblematic image which Fray Luis himself chose as his motto, blazoning it upon the title-page of books which he published after having been acquitted by the Inquisition: it is the image of the oak tree which paradoxically draws new life and strength from being cut back by the axe.

> Bien como la ñudosa
> carrasca, en alto risco desmochada
> con hacha poderosa,
> del ser despedazada
> del hierro torna rica y esforzada...

This is a translation of a stanza from Horace (Odes IV. iv.57-60):

> duris ut ilex tonsa bipennibus
> migrae feraci frondis in Algido,
> per damna, per caedes ab ipso
> ducit opes animumque ferro.

The words which Fray Luis chose for his motto were 'ab ipso ferro', which the inquisitors of Valladolid rightly interpreted as a defiant allusion to the Holy Office itself. Thus, this stanza alone would be enough to confirm Dámaso Alonso's autobiographical interpretation of our second group of odes.

Ode XII ends on a note of challenging direct address: the poet allows his righteous man to speak for him in the first person, in four eloquent stanzas (lines 46-65), telling his enemies to do their worst and taunting them with his own spiritual salvation. This is no longer the voice of the aloof pagan Stoic nor of the confident singer of Psalm 26, but rather the passionate voice of the Christian martyr, eager to suffer physically because he knows that his soul is immune and that the death of his body will release him for flight straight to heaven. (Scholars have detected echoes here of the 'Passio Sancti Vincenti martyris', Hymn V of the *Peristephanon* of Prudentius, the first great Christian poet of Spain.) These are the final words spoken by the righteous man (lines 56-65):

> Ahonda más adentro;
> desvuelva las entrañas el insano
> puñal; penetra al centro;
> mas es trabajo vano:
> jamás me alcanzará tu corta mano.

> Rompiste mi cadena,
> ardiendo por prenderme: al gran consuelo
> subido he por tu pena;
> ya suelto encumbro el vuelo,
> traspaso sobre el aire, huello el cielo.

The voice of the martyr, defying the Roman executioners, is here a transparent historical metaphor for Fray Luis's own exultation at having escaped the Valladolid dungeons of his inquisitorial enemies, who we now realize may well be alluded to in the first four stanzas of this ode: the miser (the property of a condemned man was confiscated for those who had denounced him to the Inquisition), the politician (the Spanish Inquisition was a clerical institution responsible to the Monarchy rather than to the Church), and the suffering lover (suggesting, perhaps, that not every Dominican was free of erotic concerns?). We may conclude that Ode XII is one of the most overtly autobiographical of all Fray Luis's poems, one which it would certainly have been dangerous to publish under his name during his lifetime.

By contrast, Ode XV (*A don Pedro Portocarrero*: 'No siempre es poderosa') is restrained in tone, but no less clear in its allusions to recent acquittal; it has been suggested that *Triunfo de la inocencia* would be an appropriate title. In stanzas 2 and 3 cosmic metaphors evoke mythological earth-born giants incapable of conquering heaven, and cold mists which are defeated by the brilliance of the sun. But moral innocence, like a warrior wearing the armor of truth, is revealed directly as the real victor in the remaining stanzas. The only figurative complexities may be found in the 'tigre' and 'basilisco' or 'sierpe' of lines 27-8 and 44: they are traditional metaphors of evil power, but Coster (*16*) has also taken the tiger to be a specific allusion to the name of León de Castro, and the basilisk to Basilio de Medina. The repetition of the combination of these two animals as the arch-enemies gives some weight to the argument. A textual variant in line 48 ('venciendo', 'veniendo') must be resolved, it seems to me, in favor of the verb *venir* (modern 'viniendo'). But as a whole the ode is a simple triumphant hymn, skilfully combining moralistic echoes from Horace with those of the Biblical tradition.

Thematically, Ode XVI (*Contra un juez avaro*: 'Aunque en ricos montones') is quite similar to the preceding one, and it is only this similarity which supports an autobiographical reading: it could otherwise be taken as a simple satire on the corruption of judges and their inevitable punishment. But in syntactic movement the two poems differ completely. Ode XV's stanzas consist of seven lines each; and each stanza is a complete syntactic unit, a grammatical sentence which could end with a full stop. Ode XVI, on the other hand, consists of much briefer four-line stanzas (with a final coda of a rhymed couplet); and there is no full stop until we reach the end, with line 30. Four subordinate clauses beginning with the conjunction 'Aunque' dominate the syntax until the middle of line 10; then a negative series of main clauses ('no' or 'ni' appear nine times) leads up to the emphatic coda:

> y quedarás sumido
> en males no finibles y en olvido.

What Dámaso Alonso has called abrupt enjambement links many lines and stanzas: only one indignant sentence flows unbroken through seven and one-half stanzas, envisioning the awful tortures of an unjust judge, eternally damned in life and in death.

With Ode XIV (*Al apartamiento*: '¡Oh ya seguro puerto!'), and its familiar appendix Décima XXIII (*A la salida de la cárcel*: 'Aquí la envidia y mentira'), we complete the cycle of poems that refer to Fray Luis's imprisonment, his unjust accusers, and his exoneration. The first three stanzas of Ode XIV begin with a

burst of vocatives, addressed first figuratively to a secure port or
refuge from prolonged wandering ('luengo error'), and then
more literally to a place of rest ('¡oh deseado... reposo!') which
is defined as a 'techo pajizo' and a 'sierra'. But we should not
yield to the Romantic temptation to read these latter two concrete nouns too literally: the thatched roof is clearly an emblem
of the simple life, free from persecution, and the high mountains
raise us up from the earth and closer to heaven. This more or less
symbolic mountain retreat is to separate him from the sinful
world and to give him a chance to recover and to forget (lines
16-30). Lines 28-30 are not easy to understand very precisely:
what exactly has left unpleasant things imprinted on the poet's
memory? (The image is certainly one of slowly erasing —
'borro' — a deeply inscribed message.) Sarmiento's note
clarifies the passage as well as can be: the poet's preceding life
('vivir') is seen as a mad process of change from 'vain joy to act-
ual misfortune'.

Stanza 7 (lines 31-5) introduces a new image, taken from the
opening lines of Book II of Lucretius's *De rerum natura*, in
which the philosopher views from a safe and lofty vantage point
the perils of shipwrecked sailors in the stormy sea below. This
landscape is undoubtedly allegorical: the mountain represents a
state of grace, of relief from the pressures of the world, while the
ocean-tossed vessels below represent the harried activity of men
in the world. The final figure is that of a swimmer vainly trying
to escape death by clinging to a board from the wrecked ship ('el
leño deshecho') and fighting against the waves (lines 56-60):

> Esfuerza, opone el pecho,
> mas ¿cómo será parte un afligido
> que va, el leño deshecho,
> de flaca tabla asido,
> contra un abismo inmenso embravecido?

The concluding stanza returns to the 'seguro puerto' of the initial stanza: the Spanish word 'puerto', as Audrey Lumsden
Kouvel (*21*) has pointed out, is a haven, a place of refuge, ambiguously vacillating between 'seaport' and 'mountain pass', but

clearly defined by the binary oppositions which control the semantics of this particular poem, which leads directly into the great Ode I, commonly entitled *De la vida retirada* ('¡Qué descansada vida!'). But first let us close this chapter with the no less familiar *décima*, which surely needs no commentary:

> *A la salida de la cárcel*
> Aquí la envidia y mentira
> me tuvieron encerrado.
> Dichoso el humilde estado
> del sabio que se retira
> de aqueste mundo malvado,
> y con pobre mesa y casa
> en el campo deleitoso
> con solo Dios se compasa
> y a solas su vida pasa,
> ni envidiado ni envidioso.

4. From Satire toward Mysticism

Fray Luis de León's reputation as a major poet depends especially upon our final group of seven odes, in particular upon the five that we may call transcendental. The first two are more narrowly satirical; that is, they are moralistic critiques of those worldly temptations which lead men astray from the path of virtue and true happiness. We are all familiar, in a general way, with this moral attitude, which is typical of the Judeo-Christian tradition. Our poet draws of course upon this tradition, but his primary terms of reference are those of the classical world, the myths and legends of pagan Antiquity as interpreted by moralistic philosophers such as the Roman Stoics. The Stoic school of philosophy, founded in Greece about 300 B.C., had had an important ethical influence upon the aristocracy of Rome; the poet Horace was thoroughly familiar with its doctrines. Later, during the first and second centuries of the Christian era, such authors as Seneca the Younger (born in Cordova about A.D. 1) and the Emperor Marcus Aurelius (born A.D. 121) continued this ethical tradition. The Stoics tended to attribute allegorical meanings to poetic myths; many of their ideas were adapted to Christianity by the Latin Fathers of the Church.

In Poem V (*De la avaricia*) we have a short and simple example of how Fray Luis creates a modern Spanish satire out of an ancient Stoic theme. He gives the theme a personal focus by addressing the poem to his friend Felipe Ruiz (see also Poems XII and X), whose name appears as a vocative in line 7. As in Horace's odes, maritime commerce is the primary example, and symbol, of avarice: the feverish search for wealth on the high seas disrupts the philosopher's search for *ataraxia*, or peace of mind, which was the Stoic ideal. In his first two stanzas the poet mentions, not maritime commerce in general, but the recent historical phenomenon of Portuguese voyages to the Orient (the

Persian Gulf, the Moluccas, India) in search of spices and gems. The 'árbol bueno' may produce fragrance, but does not make for 'un ánimo sereno': the twisted face expresses the anguish of the avaricious soul.

The third and fourth stanzas (lines 11-20) refer to ancient legends: the Roman captain (Marcus Licinius Crassus) whose thirst for wealth was symbolically punished by a draught of molten gold; and the mythical Tantalus, who was punished for a different crime by a similar tantalizing thirst in the presence of water. Both legends point up the paradox of avarice: the greater one's wealth, the less one's peace of mind. This satirical paradox is expressed in its most clearly antithetical form in the final stanza of the poem, in a rhetorical question: what is the value of unspent material wealth which keeps one awake at night 'y deja en la riqueza pobre al dueño'? There is serious philosophical wordplay involved: 'riqueza' refers to material wealth, while 'pobre' refers to spiritual poverty. Such antitheses give structure to Fray Luis's most characteristic poetry.

Poem IX (*Las serenas*) is a similar satire attacking, not avarice, but the sexual temptations which women exercise upon men. The 'serenas' (modern 'sirenas') of the title are the sirens or mermaids that tempted Ulysses and his fellow voyagers; they provide the extended moral allegory which gives formal unity to the second half of the ode. The first half is less tightly unified: it mentions a number of different motifs, including Circe, another of Ulysses's temptresses. The entire poem is given rhetorical unity by the imperatives addressed to Querinto, the fictional friend to whom the poet is giving his moral advice. ('Querinto' is the Spanish form of Cherinthus, a name mentioned in one of Horace's satires, combined perhaps, as Sarmiento suggests, with the Cerinthus mentioned by Tibullus; we do not know whether Fray Luis also had in mind a particular friend of his own.)

The images of the first three stanzas belong to familiar poetic codes: the cup covered with gold or smeared with honey, that tempts one to swallow bitter poison, and the white lily or red rose which poisons the soul by concealing a deadly serpent or a dangerous snare. In lines 16-18 Querinto's maturity is mentioned as a reason for becoming morally serious. The image of lines 19-20 is that of a person carefully setting his feet upon the few firm spots within a treacherous bog; this 'cieno bruto' leads to the pigsties of Circe, whose charms turned men into animals, trapping them forever. Stanza 7 (lines 31-5) inserts two Biblical allusions within the Homeric context of Circe and the Sirens: we are expected to recognize as Solomon 'the wise king of Jerusalem' and as Samson 'the conqueror of Gaza'. (Riddles of this sort are traditionally associated with moral instruction and the testing of heroes.) But 'viveza', which here must mean intelligence, did not keep Solomon from having too many wives and concubines; nor did 'fortaleza' save Samson from the feminine wiles of Delilah. The model which the poet urges upon Querinto is not Hebrew, but Greek: Ulysses, who avoided responding to the Siren's song.

This song occupies almost three stanzas in the Quevedo edition. (Manuscripts supply a fourth stanza, inserted between lines 50 and 51.) The Siren invites Ulysses to rest with her awhile and to listen to her epic accounts of the fall of Troy. The remedy is prudence: Ulysses fills his sailors' ears with wax so that they can not be tempted by the Siren's song.

The final stanza contains the moral of the poem in the form of three figurative imperatives: the poet tells his friend Querinto to close his eyes, to fill his ears, and to slip out of his cloak, if seized. This last bit of advice is a reference to the story of Joseph and Potiphar's wife (Genesis xxxix.12): after failing to persuade him to make love to her, 'she caught him by his garment, saying, Lie with me: and he left his garment in her hand, and fled, and got him out.' We see here how easily Fray Luis, with a syncretism going back to the Stoics and the Church fathers, merges the Siren with Potiphar's wife, and Joseph with Ulysses. Echoes of Horace, Virgil, Martial and Homer are harmonized with echoes of the Bible. As a Christian humanist, our poet viewed the temptation of concupiscence and the virtue of prudence from the classical perspective of a universal human nature.

Far more suggestive poetically than either of these two moralistic satires is the poem with which all collections of Fray Luis's poetry begin, '¡Qué descansada vida!', usually entitled *Vida retirada*. Poem I depends in part, however, upon some of the same satirical motifs; the agitation of maritime commerce, in particular, is of structural importance as the antithesis of country life's quiet solitude. We can read the poem as a process of alternation between the ideal of rustic withdrawal from the world, and the dangers of urban wealth, fame, flattery, ambition, power, worry, love and other worldly emotions. Once again, the Latin poet Horace provides Fray Luis's principal model. His Epode II, in particular, beginning 'Beatus ille qui procul negotiis' ('Happy that man who far away from business'), is the classical point of reference for this thematic cluster of motifs, identified as the 'beatus ille' *topos*. Horace's epode is a dramatic monologue in which a man dreams of leaving the city and going back to the simple country life. He describes the horrors of what he will get away from and the joys of rustic tasks shared with his wife; instead of sophisticated imported food, he will enjoy simple local products of the land, and a quiet evening every day. But in the final four lines of the poem, Horace gives the whole matter an ironic twist by identifying the speaker as a money-lender who liquidates his capital in order to retire and then, two weeks later, reinvests and goes back into business.

Horace's 'Beatus ille' and related classical texts enjoyed an enthusiastic revival with the Renaissance, although most imitators omitted the ironic ending. Garcilaso de la Vega, in his Eclogue II (1535), devotes three stanzas (lines 38-76) to a version of this *topos*. Fray Luis himself had translated Horace's poem into Spanish; this translation was first published in the 1570s by his fellow-professor at Salamanca, Francisco Sánchez de las Brozas, in notes on the sources of Garcilaso's poetry. All pastoral poetry and fiction were based upon a similar utopian dream of the Golden Age restored. Fray Antonio de Guevara's *Menosprecio de corte y alabanza de aldea* (1539), in prose, popularized the topic in Spain and abroad. Fray Luis's Poem I, with later poems by Andrés Fernández de Andrade, Góngora, Lope de Vega and Quevedo, represent the complete assimilation of this *topos* into Spanish poetry.

Let us examine how Fray Luis in his *Vida retirada* weaves together the motifs of this tradition to form an original poem integrated in a new and different way. (The poem is not, of course, original in the radical Romantic or self-deceiving sense of the word: like all true poetry, it builds upon and competes with previous poetry.) He begins by asserting the wisdom of secretly withdrawing from the world: the wise man escapes the psychological turmoils of envy provoked by other men's pride and wealth. (We find the only specifically Spanish touch in lines 8-10, referring to *artesonado* ceilings built by Moorish or Morisco craftsmen.) He escapes from concern with fame and flattery. In the fourth stanza there is a shift from the third person to the first, with a rhetorical question reminiscent of Poem V: what good is fame to me if I am anguished by my search for it? The imagery here is that of emptiness, the wind and loss of breath: 'vano', 'viento', 'desalentado'. The following stanza (lines 21-5) states for the first time the positive and negative terms of this constantly antithetical poem:

> ¡Oh monte, oh fuente, oh río!
> ¡Oh secreto seguro deleitoso!
> Roto casi el navío,
> a vuestro almo reposo
> huyo de aqueste mar tempestüoso.

Line 21 seems to be literal in its references to elements of an ideal rustic setting perhaps identifiable with La Flecha, an orchard owned by the Augustinians on the banks of the Tormes River; these elements will be developed further in lines 41-55. But line 22 begins to introduce a metaphor: 'seguro' as a noun seems to suggest 'haven' or 'puerto', for in the following lines we find the image of a ship nearly destroyed by a storm at sea. This image will be developed in a more literal mode in lines 61-70.

In the sequence of three stanzas constituted by lines 26-40, each stanza begins with a positive value and ends with an antithetic negative one: peacefulness balanced against pride of ancestry or wealth, birdsong against worries, self-sufficiency against emotional involvement. We may trace each image as it evolves within the tradition. Let us take the motif of birdsong, for example. Horace had simply referred to wild birds: 'queruntur in silvis aves' ('birds warble in the woods'). Garcilaso had elaborated upon this:

> y las aves sin dueño
> con canto no aprendido
> hinchen el aire de dulce armonía.

In his translation from Horace, Fray Luis had written 'cantan los pájaros sin dueño'. And now in his own poem he appropriates the rest of Garcilaso into his new idea of birds as pleasant awakeners:

> Despiértenme las aves
> con su cantar sabroso no aprendido,
> no los cuidados graves
> de que es siempre seguido
> el que al ajeno arbitrio está atenido.

The full development of the pleasaunce motif, the *topos* of the 'locus amoenus' or pleasant garden, occupies lines 41-60. Here these are no negative factors except in line 60 itself. And the positive elements are almost all traditional: trees, flowers, running water, grass, breeze. But these traditional elements are fused with a new sort of landscape: the slope of a hill planted with fruit-trees; a stream that flows rapidly down the hill and then, in the valley, flows calmly, watering grass and flowers; finally, a breeze which carries the perfume of flowers and gently moves the trees. There is movement here, and it seems to be teleological, that is, to reflect a purpose. This is most clearly expressed by the image of an orchard whose springtime blossoms promise fruit in the autumn (lines 41-5):

> Del monte en la ladera
> por mi mano plantado tengo un huerto
> que con la primavera,
> de bella flor cubierto,
> ya muestra en esperanza el fruto cierto.

This poem contains no overt allusions to Christian doctrine; yet line 45, which may be understood in terms of the Stoic philosophy of nature, emphasizes the peculiarly Judeo-Christian virtue of hope, closely related to faith.

In line 60 wealth ('oro') and power ('cetro') are mentioned; this marks a transition to the following two stanzas (lines 61-70) in which the negative image of maritime commerce is fully developed. The 'falso leño' is a semantic Latinism (see Lapesa, *23*) referring to the treacherous ship used by merchants to carry their gold. The description of the storm at sea evokes the violence of desperation which is diametrically opposed to the quiet confidence of the orchard:

> La combatida antena
> cruje, y en ciega noche el claro día
> se torna; al cielo suena
> confusa vocería,
> y la mar enriquecen a porfía.

(The last line is not easy to understand: it presents the merchants as competing with one another to enrich the sea, that is, as throwing gold overboard to lighten the ship.)

The final three stanzas (lines 71-85) form a conclusion in which positive elements predominate. Lines 74-9 evoke once more the struggle for sea-borne wealth and the competition for dangerous power. But enveloping them is a modest, peaceful table with shaded relaxation to the sound of music. The splitting of the adverb 'miserablemente' between two lines (76-7) seems by its linguistic violence to reflect the struggle for power. The inverted repetition of words from line 80 in line 81 seems, conversely, to reflect the concluding harmony of the music, an image of the poetry itself:

> ... tendido yo a la sombra esté cantando:

> a la sombra tendido,
> de hiedra y lauro eterno coronado,
> puesto el atento oído

> al son dulce, acordado,
> del plectro sabiamente meneado.

We have seen in Poem I what is essentially an Horatian or horizontal escape from the city into the country. In the four remaining odes, which are more radically transcendental or vertical, we will see an escape from earth into heaven. We should here keep in mind an important difference in English and Spanish vocabulary: in English, whether we want to or not, we must choose between 'sky' and 'heaven', two different words corresponding to two different concepts. In Spanish there is only one word, 'cielo', which from an English speaker's point of view corresponds simultaneously to both concepts; hence, given the arbitrary nature of such linguistic signs, Fray Luis can make no clear distinction between the astronomers' sky and the theologians' heaven. The reader of these odes must think in Spanish, not in English, if he wants to understand the world-view that they express.

Poem X ('¿Cuándo será que pueda?') is one of the three odes addressed to Felipe Ruiz (see Lapesa, *22*). The opening question sets the rhetorical framework for the whole poem, if we except lines 36-50, which is a three-stanza description of a storm inserted parenthetically: all of the other stanzas depend upon the answering verb 'veré', explicitly or implicitly modified by the adverbs 'allí' (line 6) and 'entonces' (line 11). The poet's present life is associated with imprisonment and 'suelo'; his future vision of reality is associated with the rhyming antithesis 'cielo' and its most distant wheel or sphere of absolute detachment. We should try to imagine the Ptolemaic universe, with the heavy Earth at the center surrounded by the seven concentric moving spheres of the planets, the whole of which is enveloped within the motionless Empyrean of the fixed stars in their constellations. And simultaneously we must see the spheres of this universe as corresponding to spiritual realities: the diabolical realm of Hell deep within the center of the Earth; the fluctuating sublunary sphere of human life; the steadier planetary influences, such as love (Venus) and war (Mars); and finally, beyond the fixed stars, the Primum Mobile Immotum, the

Unmoved Mover, God Himself. It is from this last vantage point
that the poet in Poem X looks forward to seeing the way in
which the world functions; the emphasis in this poem is more
cosmological than theological, but in Fray Luis's poetic
thought, these two dimensions are always inseparable.

In the first two stanzas (lines 1-10) the poet imagines his future
translation from Earth to Heaven, in the absolute sense. Then,
in stanzas 3-10 (lines 11-50), he will see how the Earth is put
together: the foundation or heaviest element (earth); the second
element (water) as the sea (line 19); the third element (air) as a
wind (line 24); and the fourth (fire) as lightning (line 33). Then,
in the summer storm of stanzas 8-10 (lines 36-50), these four
elements are all violently combined; this storm represents the
turbulent confusion of our sublunary world.

With line 51 the poet imagines suddenly leaving this world
behind: he moves quickly through the planetary spheres (the
'natural' celestial movements of line 54 must refer to them, as
distinct from the 'arrebatado' movement in line 53 of comets
and meteors) to the signs of the Zodiac, the 'señales' of line 55,
and the constellations of lines 56-60. Scientifically, stanza 13
(lines 61-5) should refer to the sphere of the Sun, which controls
the short days and long nights of winter; but the poet seems to be
thinking here of the Empyrean region of fire as the ultimate
source of light and life. The final stanza certainly refers to the
Empyrean in its more spiritual aspect as the dwelling place of
blessed souls, the vantage point from which the poet hopes eventually to be able to view the world.

This is the Ptolemaic and Christian cosmological structure
underlying Poem X, a visionary structure dependent upon
Cicero's *Somnium Scipionis* and its commentaries. But this
poem's poetry also depends upon its more local verbal texture,
upon words that remind us of the Psalms and Job, as well as of
Horace and Virgil. Perhaps the strongest influence is that of certain portions of Job, which Fray Luis as a theologian had
studied intensively, writing a literal translation, a commentary
and a version in verse. In the Book of Job, God uses a series of
rhetorical questions to convince Job that he does not understand
how the world was made or how it functions (chapter xxxviii.4-5

and 22, as translated in Fray Luis's *terza rima*):

> ¿Adónde estabas, dime, al punto y hora
> que a plomo cimentaba yo la tierra?
> Declara aquí la ciencia que en ti mora.
> ¿Quién hizo por medida llano y sierra?
> ¿Quién levantó nivel, colgó plomada
> en todo lo que el ancho suelo encierra?
>
> ... ...
>
> Y dime, ¿dónde tengo recogida
> la nieve y sus tesoros? ¿Dónde tengo
> multitud de pedrisco apercibida?

We immediately discover here words and concepts found in stanzas 3 and 7. The poet in Poem X implicitly recognizes his Job-like ignorance, but looks forward to discovering in Heaven God's secrets about the world. His attitude is not so much that of the modern scientist (although we cannot ignore an authentic curiosity about nature) as that of the devout Christian who hopes that his soul will eventually be joined to the mind of God.

Poem VIII (*Noche serena*) is dedicated to Diego Loarte, archdeacon of Ledesma, who in 1573 declared that he had been twenty years old when he first met Fray Luis fourteen years previously. We may assume that he belonged to that group of Fray Luis's friends (Felipe Ruiz, Francisco Salinas, Pedro Portocarrero, Juan de Grial) who shared similar interests in philosophy, which included astronomy and music, as well as poetry. Poem VIII, like Poem X, begins with the antithetical rhyme 'cielo'/'suelo'; but in this case the binary opposition is of structural importance throughout the poem. We may in fact attribute to this antithesis, similar to that of city/country in Poem I, the emotional intensity of Poem VIII, its 'ansia ardiente' (line 7) provoked by the conflict of 'amor' and 'pena'. The first two stanzas, addressed directly to Loarte, give the reader a setting or context for the rest of the poem, presented as the poet's apostrophe to Heaven: it is the nocturnal comparison of a starry sky ('cielo') with a dark earth ('suelo') which gives rise to his tearful outburst.

The first part (lines 11-37) of this inner poem is predominantly negative, as correlated to 'suelo'; the second part (lines 38-80), devoted to 'cielo', is almost entirely positive. The first part begins with a Platonic theory of the relation of the human soul to ideal reality: the soul, born to the measure of heavenly reality (lines 13-14: 'que a tu alteza nació'), is imprisoned on earth, forgetful of its divine destiny, asleep and unaware that its life is slipping by. In Plato's dialogues we find a whole theory of human knowledge based on an innate rational idealism which has somehow been obscured by life within the world of sensory objects; true knowledge is thus a process of recovery. (The same theory is still found in Wordsworth's *Intimations of Immortality*.) Fray Luis's *Noche serena* follows this theory closely, first in its negative, then in its positive phases. We could in fact separate most of the words of this poem between negative and positive poles. Within the negative group we find such words as 'baja', 'escura', 'mortal desatino', 'olvidado', 'perdido', 'vana sombra', 'bien fingido', 'sueño', 'daño', 'sombras', 'engaño', 'el bajo y torpe suelo'.

The opposing upward movement begins with 'ese gran trasunto' in line 38; this is a reference, as Sarmiento points out, to the heavenly world of Platonic ideas, given visible form by the planets and stars which are reviewed in three stanzas (lines 46-60). The order of movement is from Earth to Empyrean, omitting only the Sun (between Venus and Mars); 'la muchedumbre del reluciente coro' (lines 58-9) refers to the fixed stars. What is seen as particularly impressive about this Ptolemaic astronomy is its complex mathematical 'concierto' or harmony (lines 43-5):

> su movimiento cierto,
> sus pasos desiguales
> y en proporción concorde tan iguales.

The last three stanzas of this poem begin with the adverb 'aquí', emphatically repeated three times within ten lines. This is a special sort of adverb known to modern grammarians as a shifter; its meaning is always dependent upon the location of the first person. And in this case the speaker has clearly shifted his point of view from Earth to Heaven, which he now describes from the inside with a rapid accumulation of positive terms: 'contento', 'paz', 'amor', 'hermosura', 'luz', 'primavera'. The final stanza shifts from rational, grammatical predications to mystical exclamations:

> ¡Oh campos verdaderos!
> ¡Oh prados con verdad frescos y amenos!
> ¡Riquísimos mineros!
> ¡Oh deleitosos senos!
> ¡Repuestos valles de mil bienes llenos!

This landscape reminds us of that of *Vida retirada*, but it is no longer an earthly one: it is rather a landscape 'a lo divino', translated into heavenly terms. We may be reminded of the final stanza of Nemoroso's song in Garcilaso's Eclogue I, in which the singer imagines a future reunion with Elisa in heaven. Here we see how Fray Luis de León merges into a single new poem elements drawn from many different traditions: the Platonic theory of the soul, Ptolemaic astronomy, Horace's 'beatus ille' and, always implicit and unifying every element, Christian theology.

Poem III (*A Francisco de Salinas*) belongs to the same intellectual world, but with a new emphasis upon music. Salinas was Professor of Music at Salamanca, a colleague and friend of Fray Luis from the late 1560s on. In 1577 he published an important treatise on music (*De musica libri septem*); he had studied in Rome and was familiar with contemporary polyphony, as well as with traditional Spanish melodies. Although blind, he played the organ. We may assume that Fray Luis wrote Poem III after a recital in the Cathedral of Salamanca, perhaps to celebrate the publication of Salinas's book.

The ode begins with a striking synesthetic metaphor, that is, a substitution of one sense for another: while music may be understood literally as an organized calmness of vibrations in the air (line 1), it is not literally a matter of the air being clothed in beauty and light (line 2). And yet we all understand this metaphor immediately: it is as though audible music did have a visual dimension. And the response of the listener's soul is a Platonic one, very similar to that of the viewer of the starry sky in *Noche serena*: the soul remembers its ideal heavenly origin (stanza 2) and forgets false materialistic beauty (stanza 3). Thus the music of the organ played by Salinas, like a vision of true beauty, launches the listener's soul upon another imaginary voyage beyond the planets to the Empyrean (line 17), where it hears another sort of music, the music of the spheres.

The whole metaphorical play of this poem can be fully understood only in terms of an ancient theory involving music, mathematics, psychology and astronomy. The origins of this theory date back to the pre-Socratic philosopher Pythagoras (circa 500 B.C.), who discovered the numerical ratios underlying the principal intervals of the musical scale and attempted to find the same ratios in the soul and in the planetary system. As elaborated upon by Plato and by Neoplatonists (including St Augustine), who later incorporated Ptolemaic cosmology, this Pythagorean theory was revived in sixteenth-century Europe. It is not surprising that our Augustinian friar, like many other intellectuals of his time, should have taken such a theory quite seriously.

As we see this theory expressed in Poem III (*A Francisco de Salinas*), the mathematical ratios involved in the polyphonic harmonies of Salinas's organ music arouse a sympathetic response in the listener's soul, which rises to the Empyrean, where God evokes from the planetary spheres a similar combination of musical notes. This is what the soul sees in stanza 5 (lines 21-5 in the 50-line version of the poem):

> Ve cómo el gran Maestro,
> a aquesta inmensa cítara aplicado,
> con movimiento diestro
> produce el son sagrado
> con que este eterno templo es sustentado.

This stanza, which does not appear in the shorter version

published by Quevedo, presents the universe in the form of an ancient Greek *kithara* or lyre; the seven planetary spheres are the seven strings, or notes of the octave, which God, seen as a musician, plays upon. (In Spanish, 'maestro' is the academic degree which was held by Salinas and the title by which musicians are often still addressed.) And this music of the spheres, or mathematical ratio among planetary velocities and distances, is what sustains the structure of the universe, a temple comparable to the cathedral enclosing the organ upon which Salinas played his divine music. The human musician of the first stanza is now understood as the image of God himself.

The climax of this poem is not, however, the vision of God as Musician, but rather the response of the soul (lines 21 [26] -35 [40]) to the music of the spheres: since the soul is composed of similar musical intervals ('números concordes'), it sings in harmony with the universe. The 'allí' of line 18 shifts to the 'aquí' of line 26 [31] at the same time as a new metaphor for mystic rapture is introduced: the soul is 'drowned in a sea of sweetness'. But the word 'accidente' is still a musical term, continuing the basic figure: in the soul's state of bliss it hears no discordant note ('ningún accidente / estraño y peregrino oye y siente').

Stanza 8 (lines 31 [36] -35 [40]) extends the shift of adverbs to a shift of substantives: the third-person nouns ('alma' involved in 'armonía', 'mar') are subsumed into the basic personal pronouns 'yo' and 'tú':

> ¡Oh desmayo dichoso!
> ¡Oh muerte que das vida! ¡Oh dulce olvido!
> ¡Durase en tu reposo
> sin ser restituido
> jamás a aqueste bajo y vil sentido!

The exclamatory vocatives would normally indicate the second person, which is made explicit by 'das' and 'tu'. There is no explicit first person, but 'yo' is clearly implied as the subject of 'durase'; the subject can not still be 'alma' because the grammatical gender of 'restituido' is masculine, not feminine.

In the two final anti-climactic stanzas of the poem, the first person is emphatically present for the first time. (It had been submerged from the beginning of the poem in the 'alma' of line 7.) The poet first, in the penultimate stanza, addresses a group of friends ('vosotros') who share Salinas's music with him, calling upon them to share his mystic rapture. Then, in the last stanza, he returns to the 'voseo' (polite second-person singular) of the beginning stanza, begging Salinas to continue playing his music; or, more literally, he is expressing the wish that that music never cease sounding in his ears, or in his memory, perhaps. The last three lines recapitulate in a minor key the sense of the whole poem: that Salinas's music awakens his senses to a trascendental music, and keeps him from hearing anything else. The poet's soul, which had momentarily risen to Heaven, has now come back to earth, in a dying fall.

Our final Poem XIII (*De la vida del cielo*) adds a specifically Christian dimension to Fray Luis's poetic Empyrean. The fundamental metaphor is the Biblical one of God as a shepherd, combined with a pastoral landscape translated into heavenly terms reminiscent of the end of Garcilaso's Eclogue I (see Fray Luis's Poem VIII). For a theological commentary upon the Biblical metaphor, we have Fray Luis's own treatise *De los nombres de Cristo*, under the heading of 'pastor'. There is no reference in Poem XIII to astronomy, except perhaps in the first line. But the sky of 'Alma región luciente' is quickly identified with a pastoral heaven ('prado de bienandanza'), free from the meteorological devastations of ice and lightning. This heaven is being addressed in the second person, as line 10 clearly indicates.

Lines 6-7 may reflect imagery from the Song of Solomon (v.10: 'Dilectus meus candidus et rubicundus', 'My beloved is white and ruddy'), but the figurative and syntactical elaboration is predominantly classical:

> de púrpura y de nieve
> florida, la cabeza coronado.

A literal translation of the so-called Greek accusative gives us 'crowned as to his head with flowery purple and snow', which we may construe more freely as 'having his head crowned with

red and white flowers'. 'El buen Pastor' of line 10 is the good
shepherd of John x.11, who leads his sheep without using force
(line 9: 'sin honda ni cayado', 'without sling or staff').

Lapesa (*23*) has pointed out as a Latinism the use of the verb
'pace' in line 12, with the transitive sense of 'apacentar'. Also
classical is a phrase such as 'la vena del gozo fiel' of lines 17-18:
we may translate freely as 'the stream of certain joy'. And the
'ceñido' of line 24 is another Latinism (*23*): it represents 'cinc-
tus' in the sense of 'acompañado'. Also unusual in Spanish is the
use of 'envilece' in line 28: because of the Good Shepherd's
divine music, the soul 'despises' gold. Thus, even though
thematically Poem XIII is more Biblical and Christian than any
other of Fray Luis's transcendental odes, stylistically it has an
unusual density of classical phraseology. We can see this as a
result of the poet's deliberate syncretism, or desire to reconcile
and fuse in his poetry Europe's double heritage of Judeo-
Christian and Greco-Latin traditions.

Lines 19-20 can only be understood as an explicit reference to
the Eucharistic Sacrament. Within its context of pastoral landscape and densely classical style, this specifically ecclesiastical
reference seems strikingly incongruous; the sheep, after grazing
and bathing, are confronted with food upon a table:

> y les da mesa llena,
> pastor y pasto él solo, y suerte buena.

The play on words reminds one of the traditional Christian
paradoxes, as expressed for example in Aquinas's Eucharistic
hymn 'Pange, lingua' ('cibum turbae duodenae / se dat suis
manibus': 'as food to the twelve He gives Himself with His own
hands'). The Good Shepherd is at one and the same time 'pastor
y pasto', 'feeder and fodder': unclassical wordplay of this sort
makes us realize that Fray Luis did in fact live in the neo-
scholastic world of the Counter-Reformation and was capable,
exceptionally, of anticipating the Baroque metaphysical conceit.
But within the context of his odes this sort of figure seems
strangely out of place.

The rest of the poem depends, like the ode to Francisco de

Salinas, upon the idea of the mystical power of a divine music. In this case it is not explicitly identified with the music of the spheres, but with the music of the 'rabel' or fiddle played by the Good Shepherd for his sheep during a heavenly siesta. As in Poem III, the music is characterized as 'dulce' ('dulcísimo', 'dulzura', 'dulzor') and transports the soul. The first person becomes briefly explicit toward the end of Poem XIII as well, not in an anti-climactic epilogue as in Poem III, but in a climax of frustrated mystical desire for heavenly bliss (lines 31-40):

> ¡Oh son, oh voz! ¡Siquiera
> pequeña parte alguna decendiese
> en mi sentido, y fuera
> de sí el alma pusiese
> y toda en ti, oh Amor, la convirtiese!
>
> Conocería dónde
> sesteas, dulce Esposo, y desatada
> de este prisión adonde
> padece, a tu manada
> viviera junta, sin vagar errada.

Several details of these two stanzas need brief comments. We realize from the word 'voz' that the Shepherd is singing as well as playing his fiddle. The first person is quickly replaced by 'el alma' of line 34; thus, in the final stanza, which is the conclusion of a conditional clause implied by the previous stanza, a feminine soul-sheep seeks the masculine Spouse-Shepherd, a figure deriving in part from mystical commentaries upon the Song of Solomon, a text which Fray Luis had studied and translated into Spanish. We have here a significant link between our poet and the *Cántico espiritual* of the Carmelite friar Juan de la Cruz, Spain's major mystic poet. But here there are few erotic overtones: the dominant image is that of the lost sheep redeemed by the Good Shepherd (John x.7-16).

In these five final odes we have an essential expression of Fray Luis de Leon's poetic persona: in Poem I ('¡Qué descansada vida!') this persona withdraws from the world of politics and commerce into the peace of the countryside, of Horace's 'beatus ille'; in the others he ascends from this world to the Empyrean where he will be united with the wisdom, harmony and peace of the Universe and of God. These odes provide us with an important perspective upon Christian humanism in Renaissance Spain.

5. Conclusion

As we have seen, some of Fray Luis de León's poems may best be read within the context of his life and times. This is true of those related to public concerns of Spanish society, of church and state: the Portocarrero and Alcañizares families, Spain's patron saint Santiago (St James), the fall of Spain to the Moors. Other poems are more personal, even autobiographical, referring to his trial and his unjust persecutors, the corruption of the church, his own clear conscience and his devotion to the Virgin while in prison. His best known poems, however, seem less directly tied to an historical or personal context; they have a more timeless human appeal which is only partly dependent upon the reader's sympathy for specifically Stoic, Platonic or Christian doctrines.

Besides being a poet, which is the aspect of his life which here interests us most, Fray Luis was a university professor and an Augustinian friar. We cannot ignore the social and political dimensions of these two parallel careers. Salamanca in the sixteenth century was a center of ecclesiastical bureaucracy, remotely dependent upon both the Pope and the king, but also directly involved in municipal affairs. In theory, the university was a democratic organization in which both teachers and students participated. A rector was the chief administrator, assisted by a council of eight professors elected annually and by a complex hierarchy of bureaucrats. The professorships were won by competitive examinations (*oposiciones*) held in the presence of faculty and students, all of whom voted. Classes primarily took the form of oral commentaries upon authoritative texts. The first degree (*bachiller*) required six years of study; the second degree (*licenciado*) required five more years and various tests and examinations related to one's qualifications as a teacher. The third and highest degree (*doctor*) culminated in elaborate ceremonies, including the equivalent of a dissertation (*lección magistral*) and a series of solemn acts and bawdy pranks. In addition to the central organization of the university, there were colleges, religious orders and houses of many sorts, each with its own political organization and intellectual functions and policies.

Fray Luis was often involved in the activities of these institutions. The strongly conservative Dominican Order, in particular, which actively opposed the more innovative ideas of the Augustinians and the Jesuits, was the major factor in Fray Luis's trial by the Inquisition, a separate national organization which, though ecclesiastical in character, was responsible primarily to the royal government. It was the Dominicans who denounced Fray Luis for allegedly heretical teachings based upon a direct reading of the Hebrew text of the Old Testament, rather than upon the official Latin translation. Fray Luis's acquittal and triumphal return to his professorship, amidst student acclaim, were major political and social events within the university world of Salamanca. Our second group of poems reflects the poet's attitudes and ideas during this critical period of his professional life.

Among the subjects taught at Salamanca were languages (primarily Hebrew, Greek and Latin), grammar, rhetoric, logic, theology, mathematics, music, medicine and law. Fray Luis held various different chairs in the areas of Biblical and theological studies. He reached beyond the university by writing three works, already mentioned in Chapter 1, in eloquent classical Spanish prose: a commentary on the Book of Job, with literal and verse translations; a treatise on the ideal woman, *La perfecta casada* (1583), drawing on Biblical, classical and patristic sources; and *Los nombres de Cristo* (1583-5), his greatest prose work, in which he drew upon his vast knowledge of Biblical philology and Christocentric theology to produce an ambitious guide to the layman in all the essential doctrines of the Church. He thereby provided, in fact, a substitute for a translation of the Bible, forbidden by Roman Catholic authorities. And he eloquently defended his use of Spanish as perfectly adequate to explain thoroughly the most subtle details of theology and of the Christian faith.

During the latter part of his life Fray Luis became more and more involved in the activities of the Augustinian Order. He also worked on editions of the writings of St Isidore of Seville and of St Teresa of Avila. And he went out of his way to help defend unjustly persecuted members of the Jesuit and Carmelite orders. Just before his death, in August of 1591, he was elected to preside over the Castilian province of the Augustinian Order. All of this gives us some idea of how active he was in matters beyond his university professorship. But these other activities did not in fact influence his poetry, except perhaps by keeping him from writing more of it.

More important for his poetry were the cultural and intellectual interests of his circle of friends and colleagues at Salamanca. We have seen how the organ music of Salinas and accompanying theories of world harmony had a direct influence upon some of Fray Luis's best known odes. Although he is not mentioned by name in these odes, Francisco Sánchez de las Brozas, Professor of Rhetoric, was probably the colleague who had the strongest influence upon the form itself of Fray Luis's poetry. El Brocense, as he is known, was only four years older than Fray Luis, and his knowledge of poetry in Latin, in Italian and in Spanish was both extensive and profound. In 1569 a bookseller of Salamanca published Garcilaso's poetry by itself for the first time, in a small volume without the accompanying bulk of Boscán's poetry; for this new edition the publisher consulted a group of professors, who helped him emend the text. The center of this group was certainly El Brocense, and Fray Luis undoubtedly participated. Five years later, in 1574, El Brocense published his own annotated edition of Garcilaso's poetry, indicating Latin and Italian sources and praising Garcilaso's skill as a classical imitator. And buried among these notes, as I have previously stated, we find the first published poetic texts by Fray Luis, translations of several of Horace's odes; these translations are attributed anonymously to 'un docto de estos reinos'. This detail gives us some insight into the circle of scholarly friends at Salamanca who were involved in the reading, discussion and translation of classical and Renaissance poetry. It was this ambience within which the poetic talents of

Fray Luis were inspired and developed. And translation, that is the use of Spanish in an attempt to reproduce the form and content of ancient poetry, was the first important step in the literary education of our poet.

The Horatian ode was in fact the most influential formal model for Fray Luis de León's own original poems. There are only two of these poems which are not odes: Poem XVII ('Huïd, contentos, de mi triste pecho'), which is an elegy, written in tercets; and Poem XXIII ('Aquí la envidia y mentira'), a *décima* or double *quintilla*, written in octosyllabic verse. The rest are all odes, that is stanzaic songs, of one sort or another: Petrarchan, Pindaric, above all Horatian. Let us now review these odes and their formal characteristics.

The predominant stanzaic form among these twenty-one odes is the *lira*, or five-line stanza rhyming aBabB (the lower case representing a heptasyllabic line, and the upper case a hendecasyllable). This Italian stanza (see p.12, above) was introduced into Spanish by Garcilaso de la Vega, in his *Ode ad florem Gnidi*, or Canción V, beginning 'Si de mi baja lira' (whence the Spanish name of *lira*), a poem which is itself a close imitation of two different odes by Horace (Odes 6 and 8 of Book I).

We may assume that Fray Luis de León's reading of this poem by Garcilaso and his own experimental translations from Horace constituted his principal apprenticeship as a poet. It is clear from the dedication of his poetry to Don Pedro Portocarrero that our belligerent friar took great pride in his poetic ability as a translator, competing with his colleagues at Salamanca:

... De lo que yo compuse juzgará cada uno a su voluntad; de lo que es traducido, el que quisiere ser juez pruebe primero qué cosa es traducir poesías elegantes de una lengua extraña en la suya sin añadir ni quitar sentencia, y guardar cuanto es posible las figuras de su original y su donaire, y hacer que hablen en castellano, y no como extranjeras y advenedizas, sino como nacidas en él y naturales. Lo cual no digo que he hecho yo, ni soy tan arrogante; mas helo pretendido hacer, y así lo confieso. Y el

que dijere que no lo he alcanzado, haga prueba de sí, y entonces podrá ser que estime mi trabajo más; al cual yo me
incliné sólo por mostrar que nuestra lengua recibe bien
todo lo que se le encomienda, y que no es dura ni pobre,
como algunos dicen, sino de cera y abundante para los que
la saben tratar...

By 'sentencia' ('sin añadir ni quitar sentencia') he means sense
or content; by 'donaire' he means formal charm. Fray Luis uses
a linguistic metaphor: his aim is to convert foreign poems into
native speakers of Spanish, a language which he finds to be rich
in variety and as malleable as wax in his hands.

If we examine Fray Luis's translations from Horace (about
twenty poems translated out of over one hundred), we find that
they represent various stages of technical skill. Surprisingly
enough, the *lira* is not predominant here, but rather a six-line
'estrofa alirada' rhyming aBaBcC, a form which appears only
once among Fray Luis's original poems (Poem XXII, 'La cana y
alta cumbre'). But there are at least three translations in *liras*.
From this we may arrive at the hypothesis that it was in the process of doing experimental translations that Fray Luis finally set-
tled upon the *lira* as the most appropriate stanza for his own
poetry. Garcilaso's example, then, did not impose itself from the
beginning; in fact, run-on stanzas, which are frequent in Horace
and predominant in Garcilaso's Horatian ode, are not the norm
in Fray Luis's poetry.

Dámaso Alonso (9) has drawn attention to another aspect of
what we may call the inner form of Fray Luis's Horatian odes,
their linear rise and fall. There is no such development in his
other three odes: his Petrarchan *canzone* (Poem XXI, 'Virgen
que el sol más pura'), which we have seen to be a liturgical
hymn, or series of collects which move in circular repetition; and
his two Pindaric odes (Poem XIX, '¿Qué santo o qué gloriosa?',
and Poem XX, 'Las selvas conmoviera'), addressed to All Saints
and St James, which are grandiloquent public performances.
His Horatian odes are more intimate in tone, typically addressed
to a personal friend. If, to use a musical metaphor, the public
odes are written in a major key and end on an emphatic note, we

may say that a minor key predominates in the more personal odes and that they often end on a note of anticlimax. We see this linear rise and fall most clearly, perhaps, in Poem III ('El aire se serena'), where there is a steady soaring to a climax in stanza 8 ('¡Oh desmayo dichoso!'), a return to earth in stanza 9, and a final slight rise, or anticlimax, in stanza 10. This control of movement, already observable in Garcilaso's Horatian ode, is a major technical accomplishment of Fray Luis, destined to be influential in the odes of later poets, especially in such classical masters as Medrano and Villegas.

The question is often raised as to whether Fray Luis de León was an authentic mystic or not. I personally consider this to be a question that is irrelevant so far as the literary critic is concerned. We can not know what ineffable experiences our friar may or may not have had as a human being; even the Church's doctors are cautious in certifying sanctity. What we can do, within certain limits, is to interpret the imagery of Fray Luis's poetry. His imagery coincides only slightly with that of St John of the Cross, whose explicitly sexual metaphors, deriving from the Song of Solomon, provide a highly erotic analogue for the ecstacy of union with God. There is always an implicit, and sometimes an explicit, censorship or repression of sexuality throughout the poetry of the Augustinian friar.

Fray Luis de León draws upon a different tradition for the imagery of ecstasy which we find at the climax of his mystical poems. This tradition may be remotely related to Jewish Kabbalism as applied to Scriptural studies, but its explicit sources, as we have seen, are classical and Christian: the Pythagorean harmony of the spheres, Cicero's *Somnium Scipionis*, St Augustine, and the Renaissance revival of Platonic and Neoplatonic philosophy. (And we should not forget that Copernicus and Kepler still thought in these terms.) As Leo Spitzer (*30*, pp.112 ff.) has pointed out, we find in Fray Luis's vocabulary certain key words belonging to this musical theory of reality or world harmony: 'concierto', 'proporción concorde', 'números concordes', 'consonante respuesta', 'orden', 'sosiego', 'paz'. This imagery is mathematical rather than sexual; but it leads to a loss of selfhood, a temporary 'drowning' or 'dulce olvido' (Poem III, *A Francisco de Salinas*), which is certainly analogous to St John of the Cross's erotic evocations of mystical experience:

> Aquí la alma navega
> por un mar de dulzura y finalmente
> en él ansí se anega
> que ningún accidente
> extraño y peregrino oye y siente.

It is worth noting that everywhere else in Fray Luis's poetry the word 'mar' is associated with negative images of conflict and disharmony; only here is the fear of the sea, of self-destruction, paradoxically reconciled with ultimate self-realization ('¡oh muerte que das vida!'). Mathematics and music merge in a love-death, or spiritual orgasm, which belongs to the world of the Carmelite mystics and to the poetry of courtly love *a lo divino*.

In conclusion, Fray Luis de León and his poetry represent the culmination of Christian humanism within Spain's major intellectual community, a synthesis of pagan and theological ideas expressed in classical perfection of form. His academic career and his trial are an integral part of this poetry, even when it seems to transcend historical particularities. Poetry of this sort, paradoxically, expresses a timelessness which we cannot but associate with a particular time and place — Salamanca in the second half of the sixteenth century — seen from our perspective as members of the English-speaking world in the second half of the twentieth.

Bibliographical Note

(for fuller bibliography see item 5 below)

A. EDITIONS

1. Magistri Luysii Legionensis... Opera..., ed. Marcelino Gutiérrez, 7
volumes. Salamanca: Archdiocese, 1891-5. This is the only modern edition
of Fray Luis de León's theological works in Latin; not many libraries have
a copy, and few students of Golden Age literature have read it.

2. Obras completas castellanas, ed. P. Félix García. Madrid: Biblioteca de
Autores Cristianos, 1944. A handy one-volume edition of Fray Luis's non-
Latin works, including his poetry; very useful.

3. The Original Poems, ed. Edward Sarmiento. Manchester: University Press,
1953. An edition based on the *princeps*, with modernized spelling, un-
modernized punctuation and selected variants; the notes are succinct and
useful.

4. Poesías de Fray Luis de León, ed. P. Angel C. Vega. Madrid: Saeta, 1955.
An elaborate critical edition, with description of manuscripts and previous
editions.

5. La poesía de Fray Luis de León, ed. Oreste Macrí. Salamanca: Anaya,
1970. A modest critical edition, with good notes, bibliography, and
biographical and critical introduction. For further textual details see his
study 'Sobre el texto crítico de las poesías de Fray Luis de León',
Thesaurus, XII (1957), 1-52.

6. Poesías: poesías originales, traducciones clásicas, traducciones sagradas,
ed. P. Angel Custodio Vega. Barcelona: Planeta, 1970. The handiest edition of the complete poetry, both original and translated.

7. The Unknown Light: The Poems of Fray Luis de León, transl. Willis
Barnstone. Albany: State University of New York Press, 1979. An ex-
cellent verse translation of the original poems.

B. STUDIES

8. Alonso, Amado. 'Fray Luis de León: "Ve cómo el gran maestro"',
NRFH, IV (1950), 391-4. An important commentary on the perhaps
apocryphal stanza 5 of Poem III.

9. Alonso, Dámaso. 'Ante la selva con Fray Luis' and 'Forma exterior y forma interior en Fray Luis', in *Poesía española: ensayo de métodos y límites
estilísticos*, Madrid: Gredos, 1950, pp.111-204. The best analysis of the
formal structure of Luis's Horatian odes.

10. ——. 'Notas sobre Fray Luis de León y la poesía renacentista', in his *De los siglos oscuros al de oro*, Madrid: Gredos, 1958, pp.231-53, and *Obras completas*, II, Madrid: Gredos, 1973, pp.769-88. Touches upon many trends (Italian, Classical, Hebrew, Christian, Spanish), with special attention given to *La profecía del Tajo* and its Horatian model.

11. ——. 'Vida y poesía en Fray Luis de León', *Discurso en la solemne apertura del curso académico 1955-56*, Madrid: University, 1955 (*O.C.*, II, pp.789-842.) Concentrates on nine poems associated with Fray Luis's imprisonment and deliverance.

12. ——. 'Fray Luis en la "Dedicatoria" de sus poesías: desdoblamiento y ocultación de personalidad', in *Studia philologica et litteraria in honorem L. Spitzer*, Bern: Francke, 1958, pp.15-30. (*O.C.*, t.II, pp.843-68.) Clarifies the enigmas of Fray Luis's dedicatory preface to his poetry.

13. Alonso Getino, G. *Vida y procesos de Fray Luis de León*. Salamanca: University, 1907. Based on vols X and XI (Madrid: 1847-8) of the *Colección de documentos inéditos para la historia de España*.

14. 'Azorín' [José Martínez Ruiz]. *Los dos Luises y otros ensayos.* Madrid: Espasa-Calpe, 1921. Important essays by a sensitive reader.

15. Bell, A.F.G. *Luis de León: A Study of the Spanish Renaissance.* Oxford: Clarendon Press, 1925. The best scholarly study in English of Fray Luis's intellectual life and times; an exaggerated defense of the Renaissance in Spain.

16. Coster, Adolphe. 'Luis de León', *Revue Hispanique*, LIII-LIV (1921-2). A well-documented historical study.

17. De la Pinta Llorente, M. *Estudios y polémicas sobre Fray Luis de León*. Madrid: CSIC, 1956. A more recent interpretation of historical data.

18. Durán, Manuel. *Luis de León*, Twayne's World Authors Series, 136. New York: Twayne, 1971. A general popular introduction, in English, to his life and works.

19. Fitzmaurice-Kelly, James. *Fray Luis de León: A Biographical Fragment*. Oxford: University Press, 1921.

20. Guy, Alain. *La Pensée de Fray Luis de León: contribution à l'étude de la philosophie espagnole au XVIe siècle*. Limoges: Vrin, 1943. Fundamental for placing his thought within a context of intellectual history. The Spanish translation (*El pensamiento filosófico de Fray Luis de León*, Madrid: Rialp, 1960) is not complete.

21. Kouvel, Audrey Lumsden. 'Fray Luis de León's Haven: A Study in Structural Analysis', *MLN*, LXXXIX (1974), 146-58.

22. Lapesa, Rafael. 'Las odas de Fray Luis de León a Felipe Ruiz', in *Studia philologica... Dámaso Alonso*, II, Madrid: Gredos, 1961, pp.301-18, and in his *De la edad media a nuestros días*, Madrid: Gredos, 1967, pp.172-92. An important study of the three odes addressed to Felipe Ruiz de la Torre y Mota.

23. ——. 'El cultismo en la poesía de Fray Luis de León', in his *Poetas y prosistas de ayer y de hoy*, Madrid: Gredos, 1977, pp.110-45. This consists of two previously published studies on 'latinismos semánticos' and 'hipér-baton'; of fundamental significance for the style of Fray Luis and of Spanish classical poetry.

24. ——. 'Garcilaso y Fray Luis de León: coincidencias temáticas y contraste de actitudes', in his *Poetas y prosistas de ayer y de hoy*, Madrid: Gredos, 1977, pp.146-77. Studies the themes of Horace's 'Beatus ille', of Cicero's *Somnium Scipionis*, and of the two poets' defiance in the face of persecution.

25. Lázaro Carreter, F. 'Los sonetos de Fray Luis de León', in *Mélanges à la mémoire de Jean Sarrailh*, Paris: Vrin, 1966, II, 29-40. Defends the authenticity of five sonnets attributed to Fray Luis; views them as early experiments with Petrarchan themes anticipating the Augustinian pattern of movement from human to divine love. (For these and other attributed poems, see appendices to *5*.)

    Lumsden-Kouvel, Audrey: see Kouvel.

26. May, T.E., and E. Sarmiento. 'Fray Luis de León and Boethius', *Modern Language Review*, XLIX (1954), 183-92.

27. Rico, Francisco. *El pequeño mundo del hombre: varia fortuna de una idea en las letras españolas*. Madrid: Castalia, 1970. On Fray Luis see especially pp.170-89.

28. Sarmiento, Edward. 'Luis de León's *Qué descansada vida* and the First *Carmen* of Tibullus', *Bulletin of Hispanic Studies*, XLVII (1970), 19-23.

29. Spitzer, Leo. 'The Poetic Treatment of a Platonic-Christian Theme', *Comparative Literature*, VI (1954), 193-217.

30. ——. *Classical and Christian Ideas of World Harmony: Prolegomena to an Interpretation of the Word 'Stimmung'*. Baltimore: Johns Hopkins University Press, 1963. On Fray Luis see especially pp.112-15.

31. Vossler, Karl. *Fray Luis de León*, trans. Carlos Clavería. Buenos Aires: Espasa-Calpe, 1946. A fundamental study of his life and works by the great German scholar.

32. Woodward, L.J. '*La vida retirada* of Fray Luis de León', *Bulletin of Hispanic Studies*, XXXI (1954), 17-26.

33. ——. 'Fray Luis de León's *Oda a Francisco Salinas*', *Bulletin of Hispanic Studies*, XXXIX (1962), 69-77.